"John Michael Talbot reflects on St. Francis, his early mentor, in the light of his monastic experience at Little Portion Hermitage. He is readable and engaging. His commentary is based on wide reading, and he demonstrates a wise and balanced judgment learned in his years as a religious founder and superior. Along the way he relates the teaching of Francis to contemporary events and movements."

—Abbot Jerome Kodell, OSB
Subiaco Abbey, Arkansas

"John Michael Talbot has pondered deeply for many years the life and writings of St Francis. This book distills the wisdom of centuries old texts and applies them to contemporary life with his own wisdom, gleaned from life's experiences. It is a good read that will feed people's desires to reasonably apply to their own lives the lessons the Spirit led St. Francis to embrace."

—Abbot Timothy Kelly, OSB
President
American-Cassinese Congregation of the Order of Saint Benedict

"The oldest representation of St. Francis, a fresco painted during his lifetime, is to be found at the place where St. Benedict began his monastic journey. Both saints, so different in many ways, wanted to search for God and to live their lives completely according to the Gospel. In our own day, this desire prompted John Michael Talbot to found a new kind of community nourished by the springs which he happily presents here. This book will be a great enrichment for all and will encourage them in their turn to allow their lives be shaped by the Gospel of Jesus Christ."

—Notker Wolf, OSB
Abbot Primate of the Benedictine Order

Reflections on St. Francis

John Michael Talbot

LITURGICAL PRESS
Collegeville, Minnesota

www.litpress.org

Excerpts from the Rule and Testament taken from *Francis and Clare: The Complete Works*, trans. Regis J. Armstrong and Ignatius C. Brady, The Classics of Western Spirituality (Ramsey, NJ: Paulist Press, 1982). Used with permission.

1	2	3	4	5	6	7	8

Library of Congress Cataloging-in-Publication Data

Talbot, John Michael.
    Reflections on St. Francis / John Michael Talbot.
       p.   cm.
    ISBN 978-0-8146-3302-1
    1. Francis, of Assisi, Saint, 1182–1226. I. Title. II. Title: Reflections on Saint Francis.

BX4700.F6T35 2009
271'.3—dc22

2009021206

Contents

v

The Testament

Preface

I was a little surprised when I was asked by Liturgical Press to write a book on St. Francis. I had approached them about a monastic book. But I was pleased to have this opportunity. I have immersed myself in the sources of St. Francis all of my Catholic life. I especially love the hermit tradition in the Franciscan family.

All peoples love St. Francis of Assisi. Catholics and non-Catholics, Christians and non-Christians, religious and seculars all find a special place in their hearts for him. Eyes light up when his name is mentioned. Even those who are enemies on other matters reach agreement around love for him. Some of this is based on legend and myth, and some of it is based on fact. Some of it is romanticism, and some of it is very real. But the experience itself is very real.

I found my way from the Jesus Movement into the Catholic faith through the doorway of St. Francis. From that base I have found myself a greater lover of Jesus and a greater lover of all religions. After I read *The Imitation of Christ* and some of the books by Thomas Merton, a friend gave me a little book called *Francis: The Journey and the Dream* by Murray Bodo, a Franciscan friar. This little book changed my life. It was as if a fire was ignited in my soul. Truth was that I had veered from my original idealism as a follower of Jesus and was succumbing to a fanatical fundamentalist approach to Jesus. Where once my conversion to Christ had made me a better person, now I was becoming surprisingly inhuman in the name of Christ. It was killing me inside, and deep inside I knew it. Reading about St. Francis stirred me from my spiritual death process. The trouble was that he was a Catholic, and I was staunchly anti-Catholic and had argued many people out of the church. After much study and soul searching, I quietly became a Catholic a couple of years after reading that book.

At first I moved into a little hermitage at a Franciscan retreat center called Alverna in Indianapolis, Indiana. Then a small community formed around me. At first we began under the wing of the Franciscans in church law. It was most helpful, and we are grateful beyond what words can express. After eight years we eventually outgrew that covering because we included all states of life in one community. We grew in numbers, and became our own community in church law. We are called the Brothers and Sisters of Charity. But we never lost our love for the Franciscan family from which we were birthed. As we say, "Franciscanism is our mother, but we are a child that is unique and new." One never ceases to love a good mother, and your mother is mother for life.

In later years I expanded my studies and my experience to the wider monasticism of the East and the West in Christianity, and in other major world religions. On a practical level we found the Benedictine Rule to be most helpful for our integrated monastic way of life. But I have always said that when I find myself uninspired by St. Antony of the Desert or St. Benedict, I can always pick up the early sources about St. Francis and find myself renewed in the Spirit of Jesus. It rarely fails.

Ironically, it was the folks at Liturgical Press, a Catholic publisher founded by Benedictines, who suggested that I write a book on St. Francis. I was happy to give it a try. At first we thought about a daily devotional for an entire year. But as I began to write, it became clear that each entry needed to be a bit too long to work in that format. We settled on a simple format including reflections on St. Francis.

The book is divided into three parts: The Conversion, The Rule, and The Testament. The Conversion covers Francis's initial conversion to follow Christ more intently. Rather than one experience it is a series of experiences that spans several years up to the founding of the Order of Friars Minor. The Rule is a description of the way of life of that community. I use the Rule of 1223. It is the final expression of the verbal Rule approved by Innocent III in 1209. The Testament is Francis's last exhortation to the community just before he died in 1226. It calls the brothers back to the way of life he had originally inspired. They had started to stray, and he called them back to faithfulness.

By the nature of the texts of part 2 and 3, this book does not treat some of the deeper and more personal aspects of Francis's teaching. It does not deal much with his love for nature, his personal prayer, and his ascetical life. These are demonstrated in his Admonitions, his Canticle of the Creatures, and in the early biographies. After his personal conversion this book deals primarily with the more public side of Francis: the community he founded and its relationship to the church and the world in which he lived. It is my hope that this will help us navigate the church and world in which we live today.

The entries wrote very easily. I wrote them off the top of my head, without looking up references. I tried to keep them short, balanced, rooted in Franciscan and monastic history, but applicable to our spiritual life as followers of Jesus today. I wrote about one or two a day, trying to keep them fresh as I wrote. The point was to write this book in much the same way that readers will read it. So, I tried to write brief entries, but long enough to bring out the riches of the Franciscan tradition.

I am not a Franciscan scholar, but I read many of the Franciscan scholars, both past and present. I did not try to write a study. Many can and have done that much better than I can. I tried to write a reflection. It is based on my personal immersion in this spirituality in my personal life and my pastoral experience as the founder of our community.

My hope for this book is that it will inspire you. I hope that it may teach you a bit about St. Francis and the times in which he lived, but in a way that will make your spiritual life in Christ more alive today. If it can help the reader to this end, then it will have been a success from the author's point of view. God bless you as you read. I know that he blessed me as I worked on this material.

* * *

A Gospel Matrix

There is a basic gospel matrix needed to understand the writings of St. Francis today. All the saints lived in times and cultures that were their own. Often their teachings and words are misunderstood without understanding that environment, that matrix. In this book I do what I can to place Francis in his own time so as to better apply him to ours.

But there is a universal matrix that permeates all times and cultures. For the Christian that is a gospel matrix. What is this gospel matrix, especially as we can understand it today?

For me the central teaching of the gospel of Jesus is living the paradox of self-fulfillment through self-emptying. This is manifested in the incarnation and passion of Jesus.

The incarnation is where God takes on humanity so that we might share in his divinity. The passion is where we find life through death, resurrection through the cross of Christ. All religions teach some basics regarding faith and morality from their perspectives. But all great religions break through to mystery through the use of paradox. A paradox is an apparent contradiction that speaks a deeper truth. Such paradoxes are finding communication in silence, community in solitude, wealth in poverty, companionship in chastity, freedom in obedience, and so on. The greatest paradox is that we find life in death, self-fulfillment in self-emptying.

What makes Jesus unique is not that he taught the paradox, but that he *is* the paradox. Buddhists say that we must not just teach the dharma (the teaching) through words, but we must *be* the dharma. Jesus was this par excellence. There is no religious self-righteousness in it. It is not about my religion being better than anyone else's. Jesus simply *is* the paradox, and that way is for all people of any faith.

There is a Christian understanding of the human make-up that is helpful here. Scripture says that we are "spirit, soul, and body." Body is the five senses, and chemical and electrical aspects of the emotions and the brain. Soul is the spiritual and rational mind. Spirit is pure spiritual intuition beyond earthly names, forms, or ideas. Body and soul are bound by realities and concepts of space and time. Spirit is beyond space and time. Body and soul are created energies that can be known in the phenomenal world. Spirit is pure essence and can only be intuited. The spirit is the deepest part of who we are, and is our first priority. Soul is next and facilitates the spirit and leads the body. The body is the vehicle for spirit and soul.

The problem is that through sin, or "missing the mark," we have gotten these priorities turned upside down. Most of us gauge our happiness according to our body. When we do not get what we want it upsets our emotions. When emotions are upset it clouds the mind. Then the spirit gets forgotten and covered up. It is as if it has fallen asleep.

When this happens our self-identity is confused. Our ego, or self-consciousness, attaches to outer things instead of interior things of the spirit. When any of these things are threatened the ego reacts defensively and takes center stage in our lives. It is displaced. This results in egoism and a self that is based on illusion. This becomes a lifetime pattern in most of our lives.

The way out is through the dying and rising of Jesus. Jesus calls the old self to die with him on the cross. The old egotistical patterns must die and pass away before the new ones can be established. The illusory self must pass away before the real one we were originally created to be can be restored. This is called death to self or self will.

This death to self will and such is the matrix of the gospel. It is also the matrix of the saints. You really cannot understand St. Francis without understanding this gospel matrix. Otherwise his constant admonitions to renounce and die to self seem illogical, antiquated, and a bit masochistic.

The means to this death to self in Christianity is through Word and sacraments, public liturgical prayer, and private devotion and meditation. But it is tested and perfected in life with others in community. Francis goes through a personal conversion but then founds and lives in a community. His Rule, Testament, and other writings treat this aspect of dying and rising.

The Conversion

The Conversion

Conversion simply means to "turn around." It is also the meaning of our words "repentance" and "penance." Using the gospel matrix, we turn from our disordered ego-driven life to a God-centered life. We die to the old self to find a whole new way of living. We die with Jesus so that we may rise with him. This is called conversion.

Some people think of St. Francis's conversion as a rather quick, one-time event that forever changed his life. This is not so. Saint Francis's conversion was a rather slow unfolding that took several years and continued throughout his life. This is something much more akin to what most of us experience in our spiritual lives as followers of Jesus. It is probably true of all religions and their founders as well.

Francis's conversion covered many key events that slowly formed him into a completely new person in the service of God. This process took years and even a lifetime. These events included his capture in a war between Assisi and Perugia, a time of sickness and despondency, his conversion—which took place on the bridge outside Apulia on his way to the Crusades in 1204—from a military life of chivalry to a life of service of God, his entrance into the order of penance, and the message he received in 1205 from the San Damiano crucifix to "go repair my house." In 1206

3

came the accusation from his father and the subsequent trial before the bishop of Assisi, his encounter with the leper, and his assumption of the hermit's garb and way of life. Finally in 1208 came the message of the gospel on the feast of St. Matthew to renounce all his possessions and his assumption of the new garb that became the habit of the first Franciscans. In 1209 his first followers joined him, and he received verbal approval of the first primitive rule from Pope Innocent III, one of the greatest reforming popes of history. From then until his death in 1226 Francis followed a more or less determined course as the founder of a new community in the church.

But this conversion did not stop in 1209. Some would argue that it reached its climax in 1224 when he received the stigmata on the feast of the Exaltation of the Holy Cross on September 17. The sources tell us that he had actually borne the marks of the Lord upon his heart since the very beginning, and it only showed outwardly at this later date. The last two years of his life were his final poverty—his final letting go of everything—through the terrible illnesses he bore, even though he had always been sickly because of his intense fasting and self-denial.

Francis's conversion is also set in a historical context. This is helpful to understand. We too live in a historical context that affects how we follow Jesus.

The world of St. Francis was a changing one. Europe was moving from the feudal system to a more democratic capitalistic one. Feudalism had once worked very well in maintaining the very fabric of civilization in a world falling apart and lapsing into tribal barbarism. But its time of usefulness was over. Where once secular and ecclesial lords ruled over entire regions of strictly divided classes of majors and minors, now one could pass from one class to another through a life of economic success. Plus, the economic system of bartering with only limited use of money to an almost exclusive use of money, and the opening up of more trade between producers and merchants throughout Europe created nothing short of an economic and social revolution.

We are also called to go through a process of conversion. It probably is more of a process than a single event. Most of us experience periods of conversion that can last several years, and may occur several times throughout our lives. We move from chapter to chapter in the book of our lives. Likewise, most of us do not reach the real end of our conversion until the last years or months of our lives. It is then that we discover the greater things that far transcend the various accomplishments of our religious lives.

Our conversion also takes place in our own context. The events of our own world shape us in powerful ways. Most of these are beyond what we ourselves can even see. The social, economic, and political climate of our time greatly determines how we embrace the spiritual life of the gospel of Jesus. Like Francis, we are called to do so radically. But it will probably take on an outer appearance that may look and feel quite different from Francis's.

As St. Francis said so well a few years before he died, "Let us now begin, for until now we have done nothing." So let's take a look at the conversion process of St. Francis eight hundred years ago and apply it to our own lives today.

War and Defeat

The conversion of St. Francis began during a war between Assisi and the neighboring town of Perugia in 1202.
Perugia was still under the old feudal system, and Assisi had
come around to the new more democratic and capitalistic
way of life. Under the old feudal system a lord oversaw a
regional estate of the higher-classed majors, and lower-
classed minors. These classes were often hereditary, and
one rarely passed from the lower to the higher class. The
lords could be secular princes, earls, and dukes, or ecclesial
bishops or abbots.

Originally this system had saved Europe from degenerat-
ing into tribal barbarism after the fall of the last remnants
of the Roman Empire. But the system had outlived its usefulness. Especially with the ecclesial lords, those who were
once the protectors of the people had become rich and could
easily oppress the people in order to maintain their wealth
or power. It was time for a change.

The "wars" between towns at that time were much like
our modern football games. There was violence, and bloodshed, but few were actually killed in battle. The whole thing
was considered part of the chivalry of the aspiring knight,
and there was even a sense of good sport and fair play that
made it all seem civilized. Indeed, the whole point was to
capture the sons of the rich and to demand a good ransom
for their freedom. It was a way to give vent to the high
spirits of the young upper-class men and for the older ones
to make a good deal of money.

Francis was among those who were captured and taken
prisoner. He stayed in prison for a year, a considerable

amount of time. But eventually his father, Pietro Bernadone, presumably paid his ransom, and he was finally re-
leased. He went home tired, hungry, and humiliated, but at
least in one piece. Francis returned home ill, and it took him
a long time to recover. He spent a whole year convalescing,
and eventually he got better. Though this does not really seem like a major conversion
point, it is not insignificant. Sometimes great conversions
are preceded by failure. Failure of a dream or goal often
makes us painfully aware that we are not in total control
of our lives. That dream may be noble enough, may be one
of social, economic, or political betterment of ourselves and
others. But many still fail at noble dreams. This makes us
feel powerless. This sense of powerlessness is so devastat-
ing that it can actually make us feel ill. But just because we
are not in control of our lives does not mean that our lives
are out of control. We may not be in control, but God is! In
Alcoholics Anonymous they say that you must first admit
that you are powerless before you can turn to a Higher
Power who can help you overcome the failure of your life.
The same thing happened to Francis. In one form or another
it must also happen to us.

When I suffer defeats I sometimes feel physically or at
least emotionally ill. This can cloud my mind. Sometimes
this only lasts a few hours or days. Sometimes it lingers
for some time. But ultimately it is good for me if I do not
wallow in self-pity. Eventually, I have to recognize that I am
not the one in control of my life, seek out what the will of
God is for me, and get up and walk in his will. Sometimes
God's will is similar to mine, but with him at the center.
Sometimes it is really quite different. Either way, the dev-
astation and illness lead me to let go of my own self-will,
and follow God's will with joy. It is an important part of
my conversion.

Sometimes this period of "illness" takes a long time. We need to be patient with ourselves and with others when they go through these periods. It is a sensitive time. The word spoken rightly can be precious, and the wrong word can be very dangerous.

It took Francis one year before he was ready to try again. He would try again, and fail once more. But next time he would find a clue to what he was to do next.

The Bridge at Apulia

Soon enough Francis's sense of chivalry was stirred, for we find him on the road to serious war as a crusader in 1204. Apparently the needs of the time, Francis's sense of wanting to do something substantial with his life, or some vague sense of religious idealism was behind this step up to much more serious risk and potential glory. Maybe he just wanted to prove that he was not a failure after his capture and imprisonment.

But on the way to the Crusades something extraordinary happened. At the bridge to Apulia Francis heard a voice. It said, "Francis, which is better, to serve the servant or the master?" With our sense of the modern religious preferential option for the poor, we might say, "The servant." But Francis was not living in our time so he said, "The master." The voice then continued, "Then why are you serving the servant?" Francis understood this to mean clearly that the military was the servant of God, and God was the master. He understood that he was to go back to Assisi and discern some kind of religious vocation where he could serve the master directly. But as yet the specifics were not at all clear. His return home must have confused his family and friends. His father had no doubt spent a good deal of money to sponsor his military career by outfitting him with all the tools of warfare expected of a rich man's son. So, not giving up on him, he tried to get him involved in the family cloth business. Francis's father, Pietro Bernadone, had risen from the lower minor class to the upper major class by making trips to France to buy cloth, and bringing it back to Assisi to sell. He had become a wealthy man and had even married Lady Pica of an upper-class family from France. Indeed, Francis was named in honor of France, which had contributed so much to his newfound success.

But Francis was not interested in his father's wealth or business. He apparently wandered through town or in the secluded places outside its walls. He was searching for a further voice from God. But for a long time God seemed to remain silent. No doubt, his parents wondered what had gotten into their son? At first they probably gave him some space, but after a while they probably got very worried.

Our conversion also takes time. Sometimes it gets off to a rather unclear start. We start, and then we stop. We go one direction, then another. We get sick at heart and maybe even despondent. We may hear what seems to be the clear voice of God at times and only deafening silence at others. We want a clear Pauline Damascus Road experience, but we often get a personal conversion that can take years.

The same is true with the conversion of others. We worry about those we love. We say prayers. But nothing much seems to happen. Or we discover that what we are really praying for is our idea of what God should do rather than waiting for what God does. We must be patient with others and with God. We must let God be God. We most certainly are not!

San Damiano: Go Repair My House

The following year, 1205, God gave Francis another major word in his conversion. The instruction Francis received was this: "Go repair my house, for as you can see, it is falling into ruin." It happened through the old Byzantine-style crucifix that was at the dilapidated chapel of San Damiano outside the walls of Assisi. As Francis stared intently at the crucifix in prayer it seemed as if the lips of Jesus moved, and Francis literally heard the words.

After the experience at the bridge of Apulia, Francis returned home and began wandering around the secluded spots outside the walls of Assisi. He enjoyed the solitude. He stumbled on the little dilapidated church of San Damiano just outside the east gates and below the town. It was at this church that he would later place himself under a priest unknown to us by name and enter the ancient order of penance. But at this point he was still in secular clothes.

When Francis heard the words, "Go repair my house, for as you can see, it is falling into ruin," he did not presume to think of himself as a great reformer or founder of a new community. Certainly, there were many reformers and new movements in the church at the time that he was probably aware of that did presume such a thing. But Francis did not. He simply stayed where he was. He took the message literally, and set out to rebuild the little church.

Francis could soon be seen begging stones through town in order to rebuild the little chapel of San Damiano. This was something scandalous to many. Francis was a rich man's son. He could easily have just asked his father for the money to rebuild it. Perhaps Francis saw something valuable in his humbling act of begging and in the people's participation. Whatever the reasons, Francis began to beg, and to literally rebuild San Damiano. It had not occurred to him that he would eventually become the greatest reformer of the church of that time and for centuries to come. This was a sign of Francis's great humility.

This has great significance for us. We also live in a time when the church is in need of renewal and reform. It has been said that Pope John Paul II was the greatest pope since Innocent III. He too was a reforming pope for a reforming time. God knows there are great needs today. We also need to bring the gospel to a most troubled church and world. We face a staggering crisis of vocations to, and standard of living in, monastic and consecrated life and the clerical priesthood. We also face the breakdown of the nuclear family and basic Catholic Christian standards of morality and daily living. The world herself faces the troubles of rampant individualism, consumerism, promiscuity, and the resulting problems of poverty, war, and human rights violations. These all demand courageous commitment and action. But we should not get any bigheaded ideas.

Like Francis, most of us are just called to begin right where we are and do the most helpful thing for the church and the world with what is most immediately at hand. We really don't have to go around looking too hard for great things to do for God. Those things are all around us.

For Francis it was rebuilding the little church of San Damiano. For us it might be doing a simple ministry in our parish like bringing food to the shut-in and poor, or becoming a lector or extraordinary minister of Communion. It could also mean just helping out with our family when other family members cannot. For Francis the greater meaning came much later. For us it probably will as well. But we must first find the great things of God in the little things of life. Then we will be given the great. Or maybe we will just discover that we have already found them.

The Life of Penance and the Bishop's Trial

Francis began to spend his time around San Damiano. The sources say that he placed himself under the direction of a now-nameless priest who took care of the place. This also implies that he entered the order of penance.

The order of penance dates back to the ancient times of the church when one who committed a major sin underwent public penance. The idea was that people were given a time of public penance during which they could not receive Communion, but still came to church. If they persevered it proved that they were really serious about coming back to Christ and the church. They wore a monastic-like garb to distinguish them as penitents.

As time went by this practice fell by the wayside. But it was resurrected about 150 or so years before the time of

Francis. It was for those who wanted to follow Christ more intensely, much like the first monks in the desert, but did not necessarily feel called to join a big medieval monastery. So, the order of penance became a place in the church for hermits, itinerants, and those who embraced greater poverty, chastity, and obedience in a new, but ancient way. Francis apparently entered this order when he went to San Damiano and placed himself under the kindly old priest who cared for the holy ruin.

Francis also began to give away his possessions. The problem was that he was to inherit great wealth but had not actually inherited it yet. In other words, he was giving away his father's stuff! Understandably, this made Francis's father upset.

Francis's father was probably not a bad man, though he tended to be materialistic and brutish. He just wanted his son to settle down and live a normal life. Religion was probably also fine, as long as he became a good Catholic citizen of Assisi, a priest, or joined a reputable monastery. But Francis was not really interested in these options.

The sources tell us that Francis's father tried what most fathers of the time would have done. He tried to reason with him, argue with him, and he even imprisoned him in the family "jail" in the basement. These things were all acceptable and pretty normal in those days. It was even acceptable to beat children and wives, so long as their bones were not broken. Francis probably experienced that as well. But, as we have come to realize today, none of these harsher measures usually work. Francis's father was at his wit's end.

Finally, Pietro Bernadone hauled Francis before the local podesta, or what we would call a magistrate or mayor. Francis's father wanted justice. Either Francis would restore what he took, or he would disown him. This was the last straw. It was the most extreme measure a father could take against his son, and it must have broken his heart, despite his anger. But Francis surprised his father. He called out, "What has the justice of God got to do with the justice of man?" They all knew immediately what this meant. It meant that Francis had become a penitent and was no longer under the secular authority of the mayor. He was under the ecclesial authority of the bishop and was appealing to him. So the mayor sent him to Bishop Guido.

The story of Francis's trial before the bishop is well-known but often misunderstood. Unlike what some movies portray, Francis was not received publically in the town square, but in a private room in the bishop's residence or office. There, Pietro Bernadone would have outlined his complaints against his son. The complaints were just. Francis was frankly in the wrong. He had given away what was not yet his to give. His inheritance still belonged to his father. This bishop would have naturally sympathized with Pietro at first.

Then Francis did the unexpected. He essentially disowned his father. He said that from now on he had no father but God the Father in heaven. Now there was no need for any trial at all. Francis himself had concluded it all. As an act of humility he disrobed completely, and standing naked before them both, gave the clothes on his back to his father. No doubt, the bishop and his father were speechless. Francis's father was probably hurt very deeply. The bishop saw the light of God's grace at work in Francis. In a symbolic act of protection the bishop covered Francis in his cloak, and gave him a tunic to wear. Francis would never forget that the church had protected him when he sought to see his way clear to follow Jesus more radically.

We also slowly find our place in the church when we decide to give our lives completely and radically to Jesus. We find our San Damianos and local priests to guide us.

We join existing movements and ministries to find a sense of belonging. We also find that we have to break with our past in order to follow a new way in Christ. Sometimes our family understands, and sometimes they do not. It is rarely because they do not love us, and we should never forget that. And we often go through this process rather clumsily, as did Francis. It is new territory for most of us. We will make some mistakes. But if we go through this process with humility and complete honesty we will ultimately find support from the church. She will cover us and protect us so that we can follow Jesus radically without undue hindrance from those who may not understand us.

The Leper

Francis's encounter with the leper is legendary. The story has been told again and again. There are different versions, some more miraculous than others. The oral teaching is often the most interesting, for it carries the inspiration of the moment captured by the storyteller and teacher. The one I have heard most goes something like this:

Francis was walking a road somewhere around Assisi when he heard the approaching bell of a leper. (They were required by law to ring a bell to warn others of their approach.) The sight of lepers had always nauseated and repulsed him, despite his natural love for the poor. When he finally saw the leper he went weak with nausea. Then he heard a voice from God say, "Embrace the leper, and kiss him on the mouth." Most lepers suffered from open sores and cuts that often included losing parts of their nose, ears, and lips. Puss often ran from the open sores. Francis asked for grace to obey, blindly embraced the leper, and kissed him on his gaping and puss-ridden mouth. Instead of feeling the usual nausea and disgust, he suddenly felt a rush of indescribable sweetness. He was overcome with the grace of God. As Francis and the leper walked away from one another, he turned to look once more at this instrument of the grace of God. The leper was gone! Francis was sure that the leper was an angel.

There are parts to this story that embellish the original sources, but it still carries the basic truth that Francis embraced the leper, and the leper was an instrument for God's indescribable grace. That is why Francis insisted that the first friars be trained in caring for the lepers around Assisi.

In the time of the Bible leprosy was a strange disease that had more to do with ritual purity than it did with a life-threatening disease. It was a running, open sore on the skin, especially around the hair. Some say that it was more like psoriasis than anything else. The funny thing was that once it covered your entire body you were considered clean. It had a lot to do with being "mixed," much like mixing cotton and wool was considered unclean. God required complete dedication. Nothing partial or mixed would do.

Modern leprosy is another thing. It was this leprosy that Francis encountered. It is a disease of the nervous system that causes loss of feeling. It begins in the extremities, and works inward. Due to that loss of feeling, lepers are constantly cutting and bruising themselves as they bang into things, or accidentally injure parts of their bodies. In the time of Francis this usually caused widespread infection in their bodies, so their wounds often ran with puss, never healed, and resulted in further loss and deformation of digits, limbs, and facial features such as ears, nose, and mouth. It left its sufferers looking hideous and frightening. Eventually they died from the spread of infection throughout their bodies. It was a horrible disease, and people were deathly frightened of catching it. It is only contagious at the beginning stages, but the people of Francis's time didn't know that.

The church organized lepers according to a quasi-monastic pattern. Since Jesus loved the poor, they were considered especially beloved by God. They were invested in a monastic/penitential robe through a formal rite in church and lived a monastic/mendicant life, alternating between times in colonies and wandering from colony to colony. Of course, these high ideals often degenerated into a pious way of heartlessly isolating them from the rest of society. The latter grew to be the prevailing attitude on the part of most people.

Francis's embrace of the leper was a powerful way to get back to the original intent of the church in setting up leper colonies. They were the special presence of Jesus, and the friars were to minister to their needs for the sake of the love of Jesus in them. They were not to be afraid anymore. They were to love with that perfect love that casts out all fear.

I have ministered in a modern leprosarium. You are allowed to minister to and visit with those who are not contagious. It is an experience I will never forget. I was amazed at the faith, hope, and joyful love of those who repeatedly chopped off more of their feet in the garden and such. One such fellow laughingly called himself "Mr. Potato Foot!" I was amazed at his upbeat faith. I do not know if I could do so well if I were him.

But there are other lepers closer to home. Those suffering from cancer and AIDS immediately come to mind, or the homeless in the midst of our modern American cities. I am sure that if Francis were alive today he would probably be found living there. Then there are just those whom we do not like to hang out with. These are also "lepers" to us.

Jesus calls us to let go of our ego and pride, and learn to love those we do not naturally like. Jesus is within them all if we can only learn to see him there. If we can see him under the appearance of bread and wine in the Eucharist, how much easier it should be to find him in our brothers and sisters throughout the human family created in his image.

Then we have to embrace the leper within ourselves. Often our self-hatred, or wounded ego is covered up by an inflated ego and pride. Or we sometimes hide our broken interior behind a show of outward activity and accomplishments. But it is all a show. We often deceive ourselves into thinking that this is who we really are. But it is not true. There is a deeper self that is waiting for the love of God. Sooner or later we must all face the "leper" of our deepest hurts and fears. When we can embrace these, then we can bring them to the forgiving love of God. Then we can be healed. Then we will have embraced and kissed the leper.

The Hermit's Habit and Way of Life

After Francis left the bishop of Assisi clothed only with a worker's tunic, he soon turned up again in a hermit's garb. This was the habit of the order of penance adapted for hermits. It was a ragged habit with a pointed hood, a leather belt, a walking staff, and sandals on his feet. This habit was clearly recognized and understood by the local folks of his day. It meant that he had given his life to God in a special way. He was probably living under the spiritual direction of the priest at San Damiano, with perhaps some input from Bishop Guido of Assisi.

Francis loved the hermit's life. At a later point he had to ask St. Clare and Br. Sylvester whether he should found a community of strict hermits or go forth to minister to the people. Both told him to engage in the ministry to the entire world. He never looked back. But even then, most of the places he founded as bases for ministry operated as hermitages, and one of his earliest writings is his so-called Rule for Hermitages.

His Rule is an integration of solitude and community in what is called the semi-eremitical life. "Eremite" means "hermit." Since he balanced solitude with community it is called "semi." I like to call it socio-eremitical, because it calls to mind that he was a social hermit.

Though Francis did at times spend extended periods in strict solitude, by and large he did not accommodate the special call of reclusion, as the Camaldolese did in imitation of some of the desert fathers and mothers who are the founders of monasticism in general. Reclusion allows for strict solitude after years of training in community life and semi-eremitism. I myself have adopted and adapted reclusion to my way of life, and have found it beyond compare or description. This is not written into Francis's rule for the hermitage.

In the semi-eremitical hermitage of St. Francis all go to community prayers to pray the Divine Office. Most Franciscan scholars agree that they ate their meals in common, but in silence, though some think that the hermits ate alone in their cells. In the Rule for Hermitages Francis allows for three or four to live in the hermitage, but historically we know that as many as twelve lived in them. Half of them, called the sons, lived in more strict solitude. The other half, called the mothers, took care of their domestic needs of food and the like. It was to have the spiritual feel of a spiritual family rather than only an institution. After an unspecified time, they could switch places. Early sources say that some places did this once a week.

Francis said that "the world is my cloister, my body is my cell, and my soul is the hermit within." He also said to seek "not so much as to pray, but to become a prayer." As we know, this did not mean that he did not mandate community and private prayer and the experience of living in an actual hermitage. Rather, it brings out that these aids are not goals in and of themselves. They are only tools. Union with God is the goal. Jesus is the door.

The main characteristic of a hermitage is solitude and silence. We are alone so that we may better enter into communion with God and others in God. We are silent so that we may better hear God, ourselves, and others. A hermitage is a place where that environment is established and protected. Without those protections solitude and silence inevitably erode away.

This is especially true for more intense long-term experiences. A physical place and restrictions on noise, contacts with people, and the work that require them are a must for a genuine hermitage. In the short-term stays of days, weeks, and months these can sometimes be very absolute and intense. Ironically, the long-term experiences of the hermitage as a way of life require that one work and have some contact with people. So a clear discipline about these things is a must.

Most of us will not live in a hermitage, and few will ever stay in one even for a weekend, a week, or a month. Most of us must find this way at home in the secular world. We must find the hermit within. We do this while working, raising a family, and attending a parish church. Again ironically, this at-home model has much in common with the hermit who chooses the eremitical way as a way of life for life.

There are tools that we can use, whether we live in a hermitage or not. The first two are like the hermitage itself. We must find a time and a space for deeper prayer. If at all possible this should be done as a regular part of daily life. If that is not possible, a time for this weekly, monthly, or even annually can still be most helpful. Even hermits usually make an annual retreat!

The space is important. For the average person I recommend a prayer room, or a prayer corner if that is not feasible. I know people who use a swivel chair that swivels out to the living room for daily affairs and swivels toward the corner for prayer. Some folks prefer a prayer cushion for seated mediation on the floor. The main thing is that the space should be uncluttered and kept apart from the normal activities of life. Perhaps a cross or crucifix, a couple of sacred pictures, and a candle are all that should be there. Anything else can just become clutter. I remember a monastic saying that a cluttered cell reflects a cluttered mind. Though not absolute, this is a saying worth remembering.

Time is also critical. Scientists have found that on average the mind works in twenty-minute cycles between activity and calm. Out of that twenty-minute period we usually get about two minutes of deep, contemplative prayer. Those two minutes can really help us as we face the normal activity of daily life. So I recommend two twenty-minute periods of prayer a day. If you cannot get two then one is okay. I recommend in the morning because it sets the tone for the rest of the day. But if you cannot do it in the morning, do it in the evening. If you cannot even do that, then pray in bed before rising or retiring. The main point is to just do it! We should also have a good method. Francis did not leave us a prayer method or a mystical theology. It took later Franciscans like St. Bonaventure or St. Peter of Alcantara, among others, to do such things. These methods have been adapted to time and culture through the centuries.

I recommend using your solitary prayer room or corner where you will not be disturbed for twenty or thirty minutes. Then silence the senses, emotions, and thoughts in order for them to die and be born again in Christ. Sitting in a stable and still posture is very helpful. Slowing your breathing is a great tool in experiencing this silence. Sometimes it is good to focus calmly on a particular aspect of your faith in Jesus, perhaps represented by a holy picture. Some people just look into a holy candle. Of course, the ancient monastic practice of *lectio divina*, or sacred reading, can take you on to vocal prayer, meditation, and contemplation in a most effective way. This practice can teach you to focus the mind and emotions. But we must be careful of obsessing too much on any thought. Sometimes it is better to let go of all thoughts, emotions, and senses. Then Jesus can renew them all.

As we have seen, Francis said that the world was his cloister, his body his cell, and his soul the hermit within. Do we have a similar attitude? If we do, then everything becomes a prayer. But we also need times and places for prayer in order for that hermit within to become a reality. Do you take the time to pray in a quiet place every day? If not, then do it as frequently as you can. It will change your life for the better.

The Pivotal Gospel Passages

Francis was living as a penitent/hermit at San Damiano. He had begun rebuilding it, and two other derelict churches, the Portiuncula and St. Peter's. Some other people came to help him, and a community of sorts began to form.

About that time he went to church on the feast of St. Matthew the Apostle and heard the gospel that Jesus sent out the disciples without any money or wallet and without a second tunic. After hearing this he cried out, "This is what I want! This is what I want with all my heart!" He immediately removed the leather belt, the sandals from his feet, and discarded his walking staff.

This was a sudden enlightenment for Francis. It hit him like a holy lightning bolt from heaven. This was the pivotal point of St. Francis's conversion. After this he was never the same. His vision was clear. From then on he knew his call from God. He never looked back.

After this he gained confidence and began to preach. This was not the written-out homilies or theological sermons and teachings of the established preacher of the church. His words were very simple. He did not preach anything complicated. But his words were on fire. That fire came from the Spirit of God. He called everyone to change and accept Jesus. And people began to respond.

Soon Bernard of Quintavalle and some others came to join Francis. This was nothing formal or organized. It was just a group of people who were inspired by his inspiration. Bernard and these brothers wanted to renounce all their possessions, and adopt Francis's gospel life and dress. At this point Francis felt the need for more direction, so he and Bernard went to church to pray.

Francis was inspired by the Holy Spirit to open the gospel three times to see what God might say to them. They did what we rarely encourage today. They played "Bible roulette." They said a prayer, opened the book at random, and looked to where they opened it. This was acceptable in those days.

The first time it opened to Matthew 19:21 where it says, "If you want to be perfect, go renounce your possessions, and give to the poor." A second time it fell to Luke 9:3, where it says, "Take nothing for your journey." A third time it said, "If anyone wants to follow me, let them renounce self, take up their cross, and follow me" (Matt 16:24). Francis replied, "This is our life and our rule, and everyone who comes to join us must be prepared to do the same." The Franciscan Order was born.

What is truly amazing to me in all this was Francis's ability to hear the gospel and to simply do it. No excuses or rationalizations. He simply obeyed. It is said that Francis "was no forgetful listener" of the gospel. What he heard, he put immediately into practice. As the modern saying goes, "God said it, I believe it, and that settles it." This can be misapplied to be sure. But there is something wonderfully refreshing about Francis's ability to be so clear about the fundamentals of his calling and new community without becoming fundamentalistic. This is quite a trick.

In the case of St. Francis it was a special gift from God. Part of that gift came from his basic character and nature. He was a good person. But that was not enough. He needed the gift of the Spirit to see it through. Neither can we go through a conversion based only on our own human power, no matter how good it might be. We need God's help. God will always give it to the one who asks with a faith that is both humble and confident.

This was the pivot point of Francis's conversion and new way of life. Everything up to then was just leading up to this. Everything afterward flowed forth from it. He utterly and completely became a man of the gospel of Jesus, and an instrument of the Holy Spirit. After this he was unstoppable.

We also have conversion points in our lives. Initial conversion and ongoing conversion are processes taking many days, months, or years. But somewhere in most everyone's spiritual conversion is a special point that is decisive above all others. It may come in a low point of crisis or at a point of ecstasy. But it will come. It changes us irrevocably. We drop all we have ever been, and become something new. We are never the same.

It may come as a call to marriage, clerical ordination, or celibate or marital consecration in a particular ministry or community. It may be to live a new way of gospel living, and new forms may be founded. It can come in all kinds of ways and to all kinds of callings from God. But it comes to all who give their lives to God in a serious way.

In Catholic Christianity it is always a call to live the gospel more radically within the church. The gospel comes forth into this world through the church and is a yardstick to measure the further development of the church. Each supports the other. This is the test for an authentic call. This often means seeking further discernment from a spiritual director. But this discernment is meant to fan into a flame the gift of the Spirit from God in the penitent's life. It is never meant to cool the call.

Have we been through such a point in our lives? Many say that they have not. But if we really think back we will almost always find those conversion points that changed our lives forever. They can be good or bad, for God or for the godless world, or even from the devil. But whether we like it or not, we are all on a road of conversion. The trick is to let our lives be changed for God by giving ourselves to him completely. That is what St. Francis did. That is why God could use him to change the world. He can use us too!

The Rule

Introduction to the Rule of 1223

There are several rules of St. Francis that we know of. There is the one approved by Pope Innocent III in 1209. There is the long Rule of 1221, and the Rule of 1223. Some believe there are fragments of an interim rule.

The Rule of 1209 was not a written rule, but was known only through oral tradition. It was composed almost exclusively of Scripture, with a little added for application to the life of the first friars. This was the one approved by Pope Innocent III in 1209. Interestingly enough, it was this verbal approval by the pope that kept the Franciscans from having to profess another existing rule after new ones were prohibited in AD 1215 at the Fourth Lateran Council.

The Rule of 1221 is known as the Regula Non Bullata (RNB), or the noncanonical rule. It was never approved by church law, and served as an interim document for the developing life of the first community. It is longer than the final Rule of 1223 and contains much rich teaching that came from Francis himself. It is very valuable in this regard.

The Rule of 1223 was the final rule, and was approved by the church as a canonical rule. "Canonical" simply means "yardstick." A canonical rule is formally approved and is used to measure the further development and life of a community. Written just three years before Francis died, this

Rule is short and concise, but still authentically carries the spirit of St. Francis. It uses many of the same chapter titles as the longer Rule of 1221, but also combines some. It is not considered a "new" rule, but an approbation of the one verbally approved in 1209 by Pope Innocent III. Some have said that this rule was forced on Francis and did not authentically carry his spirit or charism. This is untrue, though it is admittedly a much more legal document than the previous ones.

It is true that there were some interesting stories around the writing of the final Rule. Francis went into the solitude of the hermitage of Fonte Columbo to write the final version of the Rule for church approval. He fasted and prayed after the manner of Moses and Jesus as he wrote. When he brought it back from the solitude of the hermitage, he gave it to the ministers for safekeeping. Apparently the ministers did not like what they read, for they conveniently "lost" it! So Francis went back into solitude and wrote it again. This is what we now call the Regula Bullata (RB), or the canonical rule approved according to church law. It is the Rule of 1223.

The story goes that some of the first friars still objected to this Rule due to Francis's insistence on holy poverty. The ministers went to Francis and asked him to write this Rule for himself, but not for them. At this time Francis prayed, and a voice was heard from heaven saying that the Rule was to be obeyed, "without gloss, without gloss, without gloss!" According to the story, the friars ran down the hill "alarmed and striking their breasts."

The tendency of the friars to rationalize and compromise the Rule persisted. Francis wrote a Testament, probably the year he died, in which he insisted that the friars obey the Rule they had professed. Francis never considered the Rule of 1223 anything other than the word of God for them and the work of his own hand. We can safely use it as a text for reflection on St. Francis today.

The Basics

Chapter I
In the name of the Lord!
The Life of the Friars Minor begins:

The rule and life of the Friars Minor is this: to observe the
holy Gospel of our Lord Jesus Christ

This is the first line on the Rule of the Friars Minor, or
the Franciscans. Each word is power packed and deserves a
complete treatment. For our purpose let's just briefly point
out some basic essentials.

"The Rule"

It is a good thing to live according to a rule of life. Most
of us have at least a vague concept of this. There are things
that we will or will not do and things that we try to schedule
on a daily, weekly, and monthly basis and such. Most of
this is just common sense for well-organized and efficient
people. It is good to have a plan for your life.

But this is not just a plan; it is a rule. It is like a ruler,
used to measure our way of life. A rule is more deliberate
and taken more seriously. A plan can be amended or just
chucked if we don't like it. A rule is more solemn. It is serious and used for a deliberate period of life. Sometimes a
rule is even for life.

This is also a religious rule. Religious rules do not change,
and only a few such rules exist in the church. After the
Fourth Lateran Council in 1215 there have not been any

new rules allowed in the church. All other legislation is in the form of constitutions and statutes that can be more easily amended and changed. Most communities after the thirteenth century either professed an existing rule and/or existed under constitutions and statutes. This makes rules even more solemn, and the community and the church formally establish it.

This means there is a real system of checks and balances in place to keep us faithful to this rule. This happens through the community and the church. The community we are part of agrees to the rule, and the church formally recognizes and establishes it. Both call the individual and the community to constantly reevaluate how faithful they are being to the rule they profess. This is done through formal meetings or just through a daily examination of conscience. This is a powerful way to keep us honest.

In ancient monastic tradition there is another rule. It is the daily schedule beyond the community rule that one puts together for himself or herself under the direction of a spiritual father or mother. For us this usually means finding a good spiritual director who will help us live our Catholic Christian life in a more specific way. In our community we ask new members to submit a daily rule for approval as well as promise obedience to our Rule, Constitutions, and leadership.

"Friars Minor"

This simply means "little brothers," or "lesser brothers." "Friar" simply means "brother." "Minor" means "little." But there is a bit more to it. Francis and the friars intentionally chose not to be part of the upper class, called the "maggiore," or "majors," and chose to be part of the lower class, called the "minore," or "minors." This means that

Francis was protesting against the idea that worldly success brings ultimate happiness and peace. It also means that Francis believed that the greatest way to happiness is to be a servant of all.

To be a servant means that we place ourselves beneath others in order to help them carry the weight of life, and in so doing we are relieved of our own heavy burden. Jesus says, "take my yoke on your shoulders, for my yoke is easy and my burden is light." That yoke is the cross. The way of the cross is complete paradox. A paradox is an apparent contradiction that speaks a deeper truth. We find life in death to self, wealth in poverty, freedom in obedience, communion in solitude, and so on. So, we find ourselves relieved of our own burden when we relieve the burdens of others.

Serving others is also practical. We intentionally make ourselves smaller than others to help us avoid trying to set ourselves above others through ego and pride. Saint Paul says, "Consider others as more important than or superior to yourselves." This does not mean a false humility that artificially puts on a humble affect but interiorly feels self-righteous and proud for being humble! The lesser brother genuinely sees the good gifts of others, and helps them to realize the full potential of those gifts. Saint Paul also says that we are "the body of Christ." We must see the good in all people, and the gifts that each person holds as their own unique gift. In this sense everyone has a gift that no one else has. Everyone is "better," and everyone is equal. Only then can we genuinely realize our own gifts as well.

"Holy Gospel"

Following Jesus is good news! It is not just about religious rules and regulations. It is about some guidelines and teachings that truly set us free. One of the essential basics of the gospel is that the old self dies with Christ so that a new self may be raised up in Christ. This is also part of the paradox of the cross.

This is a most difficult lifelong process. But its rewards are incomparable. To actually let go of the self in order to find out who we really are is good news! It is good news for us, and for everyone we know and love. The old self does not really make us happy, nor does it really make anyone else all that happy either. To dare to believe that we can actually be the person God created us to be is great news! To dare to believe that we can love rather than hate, be selfless rather than self-preoccupied, forgiving rather than judgmental, and so on, is the essence of the good news of Jesus Christ. It forms the very heart of any good religious rule. The Rule of the Friars Minor is no exception.

"Jesus Christ"

Francis was totally preoccupied with Jesus. The sources tell us that he had Jesus in his hands, Jesus in his feet, Jesus in his heart and mind, indeed, Jesus throughout his entire being. And he was all aflame to share this wonderful gift of Jesus with all people and with all creation, animate and inanimate. Some have said that he might have been a Jesus Freak in the '60s. But as an old friend of mine used to say, "Jesus doesn't make freaks out of people, but people out of freaks!" Francis was no hippie saint. He was something far more radical.

"Jesus Christ" means "the Anointed Savior." It is not enough to simply believe the right set of doctrines. To be a "Christian" means to be "another Christ." This means to be anointed by the same Spirit with whom he was anointed. With the help of the Spirit we try to actually live like Jesus. But we cannot just mimic the life he lived two thousand years ago in the Middle East. We must adapt that life to our own day and time. We may look very different than Jesus, but our heart and spirit will be the same. We do this with the help of the Spirit, who anoints us and guides us as he did Jesus. The Spirit actually takes up residence within us. We can say with St. Paul that "it is no longer I who live, but Christ who lives within me."

Some people believe that they are anointed, but they are just excited. Simply learning how to get excited about Christianity is not necessarily real Christianity. You can get excited about a football game, politics, a talent, or a job. You can even get excited about religion, and still miss God. Fanaticism and fundamentalism are examples of this error. It is good to have genuine religious enthusiasm, but excitement alone is not enough. What is needed is real spirituality that changes one's life for the better.

So, I often say that a good definition of a Christian is not just to be "like Christ," or "anointed." I say that we need to be "like Jesus." This puts some real flesh on it. It gives the word meaning that is clearly discernable in the actual life of Christ. To follow this example was clearly the intention of the great saints of history. It was certainly the complete intention and desire of St. Francis.

Jesus is also our Savior. The words "saved" and "salvation" have been so overused and misused that we often forget how powerful the reality behind the words really is. Many of us remember how empty and desperate life was without a serious relationship with Jesus. We also remember how amazing it was when we first really accepted the gift of Jesus into our life. This is the essence of "salvation."

But as time rolls on we sometimes forget. Scripture tells us to never forget our "first love." The way of the first monks of the desert was never to forget that reality. Their hearts and minds were never far from that first experience of salvation. Francis was the same. When you are always grateful for what God has done for you and remember what you once were without him, you become always joyful, even in the midst of daily sorrows, and always compassionate toward others. It is hard to be self-righteous when one always remembers the reality that one is "saved."

Will we place ourselves under the rule of Jesus Christ, or will we continue to live under the tyranny of self-will and self-obsession? Do we seek to be anointed by the Spirit of Jesus, or are we just excited? Are we truly mindful of what we would be like without God in our lives, are we really appreciative of being saved? Are we willing to be a little brother or sister Christ in order to find our true greatness in serving others, or will we live in the small-mindedness of serving only ourselves?

These are some of the questions that these opening words of the Rule of the Order of Friars Minor present to us today and eventually to all people everywhere.

The Evangelical Counsels

. . . by living in obedience, without anything of their own, and in chastity.

Here we get to some specifics about how to live the gospel of Jesus Christ. We place the battle against our ego and pride under the guidance of someone other than ourselves.

This is obedience. We overcome the rampant individualism of the West with obedience, the rampant consumerism of the West with radical simplicity or poverty, and the radical promiscuity of the West with chastity. These are radical countercultural concepts and lifestyles.

These three commitments of obedience, poverty, and chastity are called the evangelical counsels. Francis was the first one to actually list them in a religious rule. Thomas Aquinas was the theologian who said that they constitute the basic commitments of religious, or what we now call consecrated life. They are made as vows. While this is not necessarily wrong, it does not tell the whole story.

Before the time of Francis, over 1,200 years of Christian and 1,000 years of monastic history, monks and ascetics did not specifically profess these three vows. In the desert they simply went into solitude, placed themselves under a spiritual father, and lived the life. It was understood that they had embraced a way of life that was permanent. To leave the monastic state was considered apostasy. By the time of St. Benedict (AD 480?–547) in the West, commitments of *obedience, stability,* and *conversion of manners,* or *life,* were formalized. The Rule of the Master, some thirty years before Benedict, describes "vows" that are made to God and witnessed by the community. The Rule of St. Benedict describes "oaths" that are to the community witnessed by God.

Later centuries would see further developments of commitment. We would see solemn and simple vows, promises, and covenants. Some would be for communities, and some for more isolated individuals. Each has its own specific meaning for a community or movement meeting the needs of a given place and time in history.

The point of all this is that we need to make some form of commitment in order for a community or way of life to provide any stability for our personal lives. This is tragically absent from modern life. Whatever one's vocation—marriage, holy orders, or some form of consecration of life—without commitment none of them works. Without real commitment we tend to bail out of a way of life when the going gets tough. And the going eventually will get tough no matter what vocation we choose.

These three commitments have something for every state of life and every community.

First is poverty. We live in the most consumeristic society in the history of civilization. We enjoy more physical comforts now than ever even dreamed of by the richest of the rich in times not that far distant. But this consumerism is consuming us. The few who have the much deny the needy the little they need, and the gap between the rich and the poor grows wider. Eventually, the many who have the little figure out that they can rise up against the few who have the much in order to get the little they need. This usually occurs through revolution. Revolution is usually bloody. So, if we really want peace we must give up some of what we do not really need in order to help the needy. Plus, the more we get, the more we want, and the more essentially unsatisfied we become. So consumerism consumes the consumer. Gospel poverty is a way out of this self-destructive syndrome.

Next is chastity. We live in a highly promiscuous society. People are trying to find inner fulfillment through unbridled sexual activity. But it does not work. It only leaves a trail of broken relationships in its wake. It also hardens our hearts. Deep inside it also breaks our hearts. Only spiritual union with God and communion with each other can heal our hard and broken hearts, and satisfy the deeper human need for love.

One of the greatest contributors to this promiscuity is our media. Pornography has so become the norm that we no longer even recognize it as such. It permeates our media of every kind. Scripture says that whatever we habitually think, we eventually become. As the well-known saying goes, "Garbage in, garbage out."

Many of us are committed to being pro-life. But the real solution is not just making abortion illegal, but getting to the heart of the problem of a sexually promiscuous society where unwanted pregnancy before marriage has become so common. But even this cannot be accomplished through a set of puritanical rules. Again, the deeper fulfillment of divine love is the solution. This needs to be compassionately communicated person to person, especially woman to woman and man to man, in order for abortion to finally stop.

Last, but not least, comes obedience. The core to most of these problems is the rampant individualism of the West. Individualism is proper individuation gone wrong. Individuation sees every human life as a unique and unrepeatable gift from God. Life is to be reverenced from its conception to its natural death and on into eternal life in Christ. But each life is totally dependent on God and interdependent with all humanity and creation in order to exist in creation. Independence is a delusion based on an essential error and illusion. The individual is always seen against the greater backdrop of this communitarian orientation towards life.

Individualism places the individual before all else. So, the individual rolls over anyone and anything that stands between itself and what it wants. It is a major contributor to rampant consumerism and rampant promiscuity. It destroys families, churches, and businesses. It destroys societies and the ecology of all creation.

The way out is with obedience. Obedience sees oneself as part of a greater whole, and we can only be whole when in communion with God and with others. This requires submitting one's self-will to the will of God, and the whole for the sake of all. Ironically, in so doing, one finds oneself finally fulfilled.

It also means learning how to really listen to all people and all creation. This means silencing the ego and pride of our false self in order to hear the voice of God, to discover who we really are, and to know what we can actually say to others that will really be helpful.

This takes on a special empowerment when one does this, not only out of logic, but also out of love. This love comes from God. So the root of obedience is love. Without divine love, obedience becomes a robot-like imitation of real human love.

Not all of us are called to be monks or nuns, consecrated sisters or brothers. But all are called to embrace the evangelical counsels according to our state of life. All are called to embrace simple living through gospel poverty in order to overcome consumerism. All are called to renounce our need to possess people or things in order to feel important. All are called to renounce sexual promiscuity and embrace chastity in order to find quality relationships with and in Christ. All are called to silence the ego and pride in obedience in order to hear God and others and to cooperate fully with all in building up the beauty of God's creation.

Are we ready and willing to respond to that call from Jesus? If so, now is the time. As Scripture says, today is the day of salvation, and if today you hear his voice, harden not your heart.

The Church, Succession of Saints, and Obedience

> Brother Francis promises obedience and reverence to the
> Lord Pope Honorius and his canonically elected successors
> and to the Roman Church. And let the other brothers be
> bound to obey Brother Francis and his successors.

Francis is much beloved by people of all religions everywhere. Somehow the little poor man from Assisi speaks to
something deep in the human heart of the freedom and joy
we all long for. He followed Jesus in a way that presents the
Jesus we all love, not the one bound by unnecessary religious
rules and regulations. Plus, he was a contemplative and
mystic, and loved the poor and all creation with all his heart.

Some folks think that Francis was a radical reformer
who rebelled against the church and such. He was a man
of renewal and reform, but this view is simply not consis-
tent with his writings and the early Franciscan sources.
Francis was an emphatic Catholic Christian, and a Roman
Catholic at that!

Many communities in Francis's day were rebelling against
the church in the name of the gospel. Granted, many abuses
existed in the church, and reform was badly needed, but
Francis wanted to heal the church, not get rid of it. He chose
to heal the church from within. This made him unique. It
also made him very successful in his ministry.

Francis placed his community under obedience to the
church for several reasons. First, he realized that the authority of the Scriptures, including the gospels themselves,

came forth from the authority God established through the church. This authority is found in the bishops who are successors to the apostles, and the pope, who is the successor to Peter who Jesus commanded to lead the apostles and the church. This is called apostolic succession and the Petrine ministry. If you destroy the authority of the church, you destroy the authority of the Scriptures and the gospels. Then you lose your historical link with Jesus.

Second, Francis believed that the church would ultimately protect the friars from those who were hostile to the gospel. Ironically, though the church often strayed from the gospel in practice, she never denied the primacy of the gospel in her core teaching. The church has remained a home for radical gospel communities that retain the humility to work with others, rather than claiming an exclusivist understanding of how to follow Jesus. Francis was graced with this humility. So, the church stood by Francis and the Franciscans, and has protected them ever since.

Apostolic succession is fundamental for a correct understanding of the authority of the Catholic Church. But there is another kind of succession in the church. It is the succession of the saints. This succession does not depend on any visible line of succession. It is established directly by God through the Holy Spirit who "blows where it wills." This succession can be given to laity as well as clergy, women as well as men. Francis was one such man. He was not a bishop or even a priest. Yet he became a leader of all.

Francis wanted the friars to promise obedience to him and his successors. Such succession in monastic communities is well-known. Some founders, such as St. Antony of the Desert, lived a solitary life and paid little attention to who was to be their successor. Community had only formed accidentally in the first place. All he really wanted was to be a hermit. The colony of hermits around him was a force of the Spirit of God, and he had little to do with it. But St. Pachomius intentionally founded a community. It was called the Koinonia, the "fellowship," and is the basis for cenobitic monastic communities. "Cenobite" comes from the Latin meaning "member of a community," based on the Greek *koinonia*. Pachomius was mindful of establishing his successor. This is the model that was used by the Rule of the Master in the West. Saint Benedict had the monks elect his successor. Francis did this as well.

But the real beauty of this teaching in the Rule is the concept of obedience itself. The root of obedience is "to listen." When we let go of our ego and pride, we can learn to listen to God and to people. When we let go of the need to have our own opinions and ideas be right, then we can really hear what others have to say. First, we can hear what they say before we formulate our answers and objections. Second, when our false self dies and becomes silent, then we can discover our deeper spirit. When we discover our deeper spirit, then we can learn to hear the spirit of those around us, whether they are in touch with their own spirit or not. This begins with leaders, but reaches out to all people everywhere. In a way, religious obedience to superiors is just practice for learning listening obedience with all people and all creation. This obedience revolutionizes our lives.

Are we really obedient? Many of us continue in self-will, albeit disguised under religious clothes. Furthermore, are we really good listeners? Many of us follow the outer teachings of the church, community, or ministry, but inwardly grumble and groan. We must learn to silence our ego and pride. We must learn to die with Christ. Then we can really hear what is being said by God and by people. Then we can really be reborn and discover our deepest self beyond mere bodily senses, emotions, or thoughts. We can discover our spirits. Then we will discover that real obedience does not enslave us to others. It sets us free! This is the real goal of the obedient life.

It also awakens us to the beauty of the church and the entire monastic and Franciscan traditions. Do we really appreciate and love these, or do we just tolerate them as part of our heritage? Rather than archaic relics from the past they become a connection to timeless and living truths, ever ancient, ever new. It awakens us so we can build on the past, living in the present, and building toward a better future. It awakens in us a sense of divine mystery and the sacred. This starts with the church and works out to every human being and all of creation. It revolutionizes our whole way of life in a most wonderful way. It makes all things sacred.

This is one of the greatest beauties of really understanding the church. I hope and pray that you can realize it in your life today.

Renunciation

. . . let the ministers speak to them the words of the holy Gospel (cf. Mt 19:21) that they should go and sell all that belongs to them and strive to give it to the poor.

These simple words echo the words of Christ to his disciples. There is a tradition of renunciation of one's possessions among all the great spiritual traditions of the world. Hinduism, Buddhism, Taoism, and even the Sufis of Islam and the Essenes of Judaism all required it. Jesus was no exception. The monastic tradition of Christianity continued this requirement. Saint Francis emphasized it with a special zeal, so much so that he is known as the *poverello*, or the little poor man of Assisi.

Why this emphasis? God created the world as good, and the use of the world's goods are necessary not only for our survival but also for our enjoyment of life itself. The problem is that we sometimes enjoy them too much. God wants to meet our needs, and even provides some of our wants. But when we think that we need the things we only want, then we have become addicted. Plus, habitually indulging our wants steals from the needy. This in turn leads to violence, war, and death. It has been said that if you have a roof over your head, clothes on your back, and enough food for the day you are among the top 8 percent of the world's population. This is a sobering thought. Renunciation of possessions is a good way to simplify one's life, break this consumeristic addiction, and become instruments of healing and peace.

I often think of that initial renunciation as something like diving into a swimming pool at the beginning of a race. That dive has to be done with great energy and effort in order to create the momentum we need for good swimming. The same is true of renouncing possessions. Sometimes we just have to take the leap, and get rid of our "stuff." We cannot put it off or rationalize too much, or we will simply never do it. It is really very simple, but it takes great courage. Most of the stuff we accumulate we do not really need anyway.

We are to distinguish between our wants and our needs. By constantly satisfying our wants we steal from and kill the needy. But God also wants to give us some of our wants. He is a God of love, and wants to make us happy. The problem is that we often think that we need the things we only want. This means that we are addicted. The only way to break an addiction is to make a radical break. Sometimes we just have to go cold turkey.

We do not want to be fanatical about this. We want to be radical, but not fanatical. The word "radical" has the same root meaning as "radish." It just means "rooted." A radical is rooted deep in the gospel of Jesus and the way of the saints. A fanatic simply mimics these things without understanding their real meaning. Often, religious people get so fanatical about poverty that they lose the real meaning behind religious poverty: freedom and joy.

So it is okay to have some things we do not absolutely need. God wants to give us some of our wants. Monks, nuns, consecrated brothers and sisters make a free to choice to live this out in a very specialized way. But even in religious communities we can keep a few family mementos and such and a few things that just make us happy. It was not always that way, but most communities allow it today. Lay folks have greater daily freedom of discretion in how this gets played out. But we all need to make a radical break if we are to really let go of our addictions to consumerism. As Francis cried out in the movie *Brother Sun, Sister Moon*, "Give it all away! It will only make you miserable. Look at my poor father!" Though not entirely accurate historically, it is good advice.

But there is something even more personal and challenging about it. Jesus requires that we renounce not only external possessions. That's the easy part! He also requires that we renounce our very selves. That can be pretty tough! This is because the self that we have usually allowed ourselves to become is very deeply ingrained in us. It is out of order and unhealthy to ourselves and to others. It is not the self that God created us to be, but a self we have allowed ourselves to become. Sadly, the two are not the same. Instead of existing spirit, soul, and body as Scripture describes, we have put the body first, enslaving the senses, emotions, and mind of the soul, and forgetting the intuitive faculty of the spirit altogether. This leads to all kinds of disorder and sin, or missing the mark, of God's beautiful plan for our life and all creation.

Renunciation of one's possessions is a way to begin the process of the renunciation of self. But it is only a beginning. The greater renunciation comes from learning to give up one's ego and pride in a life of listening obedience to God, the church, one's religious leaders, and all our brothers and sisters in Christ.

Do we use our possessions as gifts from God, or are we possessed by our possessions? Do the things we consume consume us? Do we use our possessions to set the needy free, or do they enslave us ourselves?

The way out of this terrible poverty is by embracing the gospel poverty of Jesus. We must let go of everything we own: every possession, every relationship, and our very selves. Those of different states of life do this in different external ways, but all must do it inwardly. No one is exempt from this absolute call of Jesus Christ. And the only way to do it is just to do it!

It starts by releasing every material possession for the sake of God and of others. Then it works to a more profound and deeper inner poverty of spirit. The first sets our body free. The second sets our soul free. We renounce our ego and pride that tries to possess not only things but also other people. When we can let go of our ego and pride, then we can let go of the need to possess others. Then living relationships can really be born again. This is real freedom.

Are you ready for this freedom? If so, then the words of Evagrius Ponticus are fitting, "Renounce all to gain everything."

Simple Clothing

> "And those who have already promised obedience may
> have one tunic with a hood, and, if they wish, another
> without a hood. And those who are forced by necessity
> may wear shoes. And let all the brothers wear poor clothes,
> and let them mend them with pieces of sackcloth or other
> material, with the blessing of God. I admonish and exhort
> them not to look down or pass judgment on those people
> whom they see wearing soft and colorful clothing and
> enjoying the choicest food and drink; instead, each must
> criticize and despise himself.

When one renounces one's possessions and one's very
self, a new garb signifying that transition is customary
among the various religious and monastic traditions of
the world. Christianity is no exception. Clothes are very
personal, and to change the way you look and dress gets
right to one's self identity. Some complain about this. But
when we get a new job we are often required to dress in
a particular way, a way we might not personally choose
for ourselves. I guess changing the way we dress for God
is not such a bad deal!

The garb of the monk or friar, called the habit, has been
a subject of discussion since Vatican II encouraged us to go
back to the beginning charism of each community. In the
East they say, "The habit makes the monk." In the West we
usually say, "The monk makes the habit." Both are probably true.

The habit is a silent reminder to the one who wears it, and
to those who see them, about a call to something more than

what is minimally required. It is a sacramental, mystical, and constant reminder to live the radical gospel and contemplative life in Christ. It reminds us all to always look for that deeper call and reminds us that some in our midst have given up everything to follow a more externally intense way. Though not all are called to that same outward expression of religious commitment, it does remind us that each of us must also do this in our own way according to our state of life. It is meant as a call and an encouragement for all. In the Far East, Buddhist monks are told that they are never to be out of their monastic robes for more than three days. They are on to something we have almost lost in the West.

But wearing a habit without living up to its significance is scandalous. Many people have negative images of the religious habit because those who have worn them have acted like hypocrites. I must admit that I have not always lived up to the habit I wear. Sometimes I intentionally do not wear it if it will be misunderstood. I do not wear the habit when I go out to eat socially or go to a movie anywhere other than in my own town where everyone knows me. But then I have to ask myself if I should really be going out to eat or to a particular movie if I cannot wear my habit there. It causes me to evaluate my actions whether I wear it or not. In the end we should learn to be comfortable in the habit and out of the habit, and we should be willing to wear it as our normal daily clothing in the monastery.

The garb of the monk or friar was to be simple and poor, but separate enough to be recognizable as a distinct religious garb. It was to be simple enough to be able to do daily work while wearing it or given to the poor when discarded. But it was clearly recognizable as the garb of a monk. It has differed in appearance in different cultures and times. With some humor we must admit that, despite the simple ideal, the actual practice of the religious habit can get rather complicated!

The study of the monastic habit is sometimes inspirational, sometimes humorous, and sometimes downright bizarre. But most of it made some sense in its own day and time. Briefly, the monks of the desert probably wore short linen tunics with leather mantles and hoods patterned after the headdress of infants. In the typical Orthodox monastery on Athos most follow a more Greek pattern, with an inner tunic, outer robe called a schema, and a conical hat with a veil constituting their cowl. Coptic monks and other Eastern monks wear a small, tightly fit, beautifully ornamented hood. In the West Benedictine monks wear tunics with scapulars with hoods and a full outer cowl with a hood in formal choir. The scapular was originally just an apron used during work. The hood was functional but also reminds us to be childlike since it was originally the headdress of infants. Sisters in the West wore the veil, much like most of the women of their time, except it was much simpler. Rather elaborate designs came much later. In the East they still wear simple veils from their own culture.

Francis adopted the garment of a penitent/hermit after his initial conversion. This was a rough tunic with an attached pointed hood, a leather belt, sandals, and a walking staff. When he received his final inspiration of complete poverty he exchanged the leather belt for a simple cord, or rope, and discarded his sandals and walking staff. The sisters wore a veil instead of the cowl.

Today most of us are content with simple clothing with religious significance. The rather complicated dress of past cultures seems out of date for us, but our culture still only understands the symbolism of traditional monasticism. Many have given up the habit altogether or only when in choir and ministry at most. Some have tried new garments like cowled tunic/shirts. Many sisters in the West have given up the veil. Yet, most successful new communities have almost universally adopted the traditional habit as their daily clothing. The public "gets it" and is responding. So do the members of the new communities.

The message for the average layperson is still profound. Dress simply, functionally, and in a way that reflects our religious convictions. This means avoiding fashion for fashion's sake. The lustful styles of our sexually promiscuous culture are clearly out of place. But we are not forbidden to look nice, and most of us are still aware of how we look to others. Many of us still have to be well-dressed in the workplace. Our clothing should be given to the poor when we outgrow it or when it wears out. Furthermore, we are encouraged to wear a cross, crucifix, or other religious symbols that are appropriate and in good taste.

There is one last warning in this part of the Rule that applies not only to clothing but also to all aspects of a more intense gospel way of life. We are not to look down on those who do not share our way of life. The religious poor are not to judge the rich, and so on. Those involved in peace and justice works, for instance, are not to inwardly judge the rich who often unknowingly oppress the poor. That would be religious self-righteousness and still an operation of the ego, albeit under a religious guise. No. We are to love all people, rich and poor, oppressed and oppressor. Only with this egoless love will we win all people to Christ.

Gradual Stages

Chapter II
*Those who wish to embrace this life
and how they should be received*

If there are any who wish to accept this life and come to
our brothers . . . let the ministers speak to them the words
of the holy Gospel (cf. Mt 19:21) that they should go and
sell all that belongs to them and strive to give it to the poor.
If they cannot do this, their good will suffices. . . . Then
they may be given the clothes of probation. . . . When
the year of probation is ended, let them be received into
obedience, whereby they promise to observe this life and
rule always.

The practice of the first Franciscans was to receive new
brothers into permanent commitment immediately. The
movement was young, and there was a momentum and
excitement that was contagious. Everyone wanted to join
in! But this proved to be an unsustainable practice. After
receiving some unworthy candidates too soon and having
many depart despite the lifetime commitment, the church
recommended a probation period for new members to see
if they were really called to join the community or if they
were just caught up in the initial excitement of the moment.
The Rule of St. Benedict, centuries before, prescribes a one-
year novitiate, or probationary period. The Franciscans very
quickly adopted something similar.

Such graduations into serious commitments are wise.
Even when accepting Jesus and joining the church through
baptism, one first goes through a year of teaching and

preparation called a catechumenate. It has been that way since the earliest days of the church. Likewise, serious marriage preparation is considered necessary in today's more precarious marital environment.

Hermits go through a lengthy period of testing for many years in community life before being allowed periods of greater solitude. Only after great discernment are they allowed the complete solitude of religious reclusion. If it had not been for thirty years of community life and the discipline of living, praying, and ministering with others, I would not have had the personal discipline necessary to handle the hours of "solo" time in the hermitage day in and day out. Without this training one can easily lose his or her way in such intensive solitude.

Even in the secular world, I had to diligently study and practice music for years before discovering my own sound and eventually enjoying a successful solo music ministry. It took years of practicing other people's music and literally shedding blood, sweat, and tears before my own "voice" blossomed almost on its own. After years of practice, making my own music became almost second nature for me.

Spiritual direction is a good tool in this. For those seriously following the spiritual life a good spiritual director is a great help. As the old saying goes, "Better a good spiritual director than no spiritual director, but better no spiritual director than a bad one!" If you can find a good one, you have found pure gold, and no better gift can be given you in life. If you cannot, better to stick with the basic teaching of the church and reading the classics of spiritual life.

The good spiritual director is only there to help the spiritual seeker find his or her own way on the spiritual life. That way is often replete with both obvious and subtle pitfalls and dangers. The good spiritual director helps one to avoid them by drawing on his or her own experience. This is the way of the spiritual father or mother and elder. The reward of finding the goal is beyond compare. The spiritual director will usually not lead the seeker too quickly on the spiritual path. They will discern when one is ready for the next step. So one goes through a novitiate of sorts when following the teaching of a good spiritual director.

The trick with all of this is to find the balance between taking our time for good discernment and not dragging our feet. We must be cautious, but not hesitant. If we rush forward without good discernment we can often end up in real spiritual trouble. If we are too "discerning" we may never move forward at all. Then we will end up at the end of our days wondering why we never really tried to achieve our greater spiritual goals of life.

Are we patient with the gradual stages of life? We must not get discouraged and give up! Slow and steady progress will accomplish great things in the end. We must be patient when we are in the process ourselves. We may want to be professed or ordained now! But that does not mean we are ready. We may want the top position at our job now! But that does not mean we deserve it yet. Be humble. Be patient. Great things await those who are willing to go humbly through the process that everyone else must go through as well.

We must also be patient with the progress of others. Some move slower than others. But they can get there! When a family member seems slow in really giving up their worldly ways, be patient. When a community member seems stuck in egoism and pride, be patient. When a coworker seems to be dull in comprehending their job, be patient. All that matters is that one is making progress. This is especially true when viewing one's progress in following Christ, living a life as his disciple, and doing his work and ministry here on earth.

Family and Religious Training

> If there are any who wish to accept this life and come to
> our brothers, let them send them to the ministers provin-
> cial, to whom and to no other is permission granted for
> receiving brothers. The ministers should diligently exam-
> ine them concerning the Catholic faith and the sacraments
> of the Church.

In times past it was believed that good formation for religious life started with being raised in a good spiritual family.
Religious training has been important for the children of all
the world's great religions. Jews were trained intensely before their bar mitzvah. Hindus considered religious training
under a guru most important for the Brahmin child before
marriage or monastic life. Catholic education and a good
Catholic family were once considered a great foundation in
making a more intense religious commitment as an adult.

But there are also examples of those who wanted to
follow Jesus, but had no formal Christian training before
coming to monastic life. Saint Pachomius allowed for
those not yet baptized to join the monastic community as
new participants. They were still catechumens, but they
were allowed to come and live the monastic life, which
taught them about life in Christ and helped them enter
the church. Today most communities require that one be
a Catholic for at least two years before entering a monastic
or more intense community life. But there are ways to par-
ticipate with a community before formal candidacy and
membership. I myself am a product of such kindness by
Franciscan friars.

A rather typical pattern in the lives of many saints is living a secular and godless life before serious religious commitment. Saint Augustine is a great example of one who lived a very worldly life before his conversion, and he even followed a heretical form of Christianity before becoming fully Catholic. Saint Francis himself lived a worldly life before his conversion, even though he was raised a Catholic and received a typical Catholic education for his day. Especially in today's rather irreligious society many still fit that category.

Today we can no longer assume that those coming to more intense gospel life have been well prepared through a solid family and education. Those days are long gone. Consequently, many who want to follow a more radical gospel life lack many foundational tools that will make that way of life easier. The family images of mother or father, sister or brother are often negative, or lacking altogether. They often carry emotional baggage that makes community relationships with members or those in authority almost impossible.

These things have to be honestly faced and admitted. Good community relationships can often reform negative family images or supply those completely lacking. But often they must be dealt with before coming to community in order for any new relationships to even have a chance to succeed. This can take time, and be nearly impossible for many. The sad fact is that many seeking a celibate way of life in the West are not well formed as human beings before they come to monastic or consecrated community life.

A leading cardinal in Rome once told me that he thought that our inclusion of families in our integrated monasticism of celibates and families was one of God's ways to renew basic Catholic family life according to simple gospel values. He believed that from those families more solid celibate vocations would be birthed. When I consider our simple way of life and how happy the children from our monastic families are, I think that he may be on to something.

Do we properly screen candidates to our new communities? In our eagerness to receive enthusiastic members, we sometimes receive ill-prepared ones. On the other hand, sometimes we kill the enthusiasm of candidates through too much screening and caution. The most ancient monastic traditions call for almost inhumane treatment of candidates for our way of life by keeping them outside the monastery door for days on end. If they had the faith and fortitude to persevere without leaving, then they were considered to maybe have what it takes to make it in monastic life.

And what about family training? Do we really raise our children with solid Catholic teaching anymore, or have we so watered down the gospel that it no longer has any taste to it at all? Such blandness seems easier, but it does not build the faith of our children.

What about parents? Often religious training at church challenges the faith and practice of the parents as much as it does the kids. Are we parents really willing to support the teaching of the church to which we entrust the religious training of our children? Or are we like the politicians who send their own children to Catholic schools while opposing the teaching of the church in the public forum and denying that same privilege to other families not quite so well off? One such basic area for parents is in simply staying together, as many of the marriage ceremonies say, "in good times and in bad, in sickness and in health." Except in the case of the physical and emotional abuse of children and spouse, divorce is almost always the worst option. This would provide spiritual, emotional, and mental stability to our children that cannot be established almost any way else.

Finally, are we willing to give everyone the opportunity to follow Jesus radically in a community where life is especially consecrated to God? No matter how bad the family and emotional environment from which they come, the truly sincere soul can be healed and make it in this special way of life. Except in the most extreme cases, we must give everyone a chance. That is what Jesus did.

The Divine Office

Chapter III
The Divine Office and Fasting and
The way the Brothers should go about the world

The clerical [brothers] shall celebrate the Divine Office according to the rite of the holy Roman Church, except for the Psalter, for which reason they may have breviaries.

Some view Francis as a kind of "hippie saint" who rebelled against the church, liturgical prayer, the sacraments, and so on. Nothing could be further from the truth. Francis was a man of the gospel. Some even called him an "alter Christus," another Christ. But Francis was also a most faithful son of the church. When others were breaking away from the church in an attempt to live the gospel of Jesus more radically, Francis sought to renew the church because he lived the gospel so radically. He was radical, but not fanatical. He conserved the fundamentals of the gospel without becoming a fundamentalist.

One area where that is most obvious was his love for the Divine Office, the official prayer of the church. The Divine Office is a division of the psalms and other Scriptures throughout the year on a one-month rotation more or less. Back then it was generally much longer, and the rotation of the entire Psalter was weekly. It has come to us through a long history, and many monastic communities still pray their own version of it today. Because they traveled, the early Franciscans developed a brief version of the monastic Office called a breviary. This had a significant influence on the development of the Roman Office. Most communities of consecrated life and parish communities pray the Roman Office today.

Francis wanted his brothers to pray the Divine Office even when traveling on the road during ministry. It formed a major discipline of their day, whether in a hermitage, friary, or while traveling. They were not just supposed to pray it individually or privately. They were to pray it with the other brothers even when not in a church. They almost always traveled in groups of two or more. Francis used to say that if we take intentional time every day for the body to eat, then we should take intentional time every day for spiritual nourishment.

For me the Divine Office has become a powerful prayer discipline for my day. The same is true of the daily Mass readings. I find it interesting that many Christians, Catholic and non-Catholic alike, are looking for daily devotionals to get them through the Bible in one year. As a Catholic Christian I have found the gift of the Scriptures already given in the daily readings and prayers of the Divine Office and Mass. I am very grateful that I do not have to go looking for something that has already been given from ancient times for us today. There is no need to reinvent the wheel.

But there is more. In charismatic prayer meetings and Jesus Movement church gatherings in my past, we often struggled to put together a form of worship that was both structured and free for individual participation. I found that balance in the Divine Office and Mass when properly celebrated and prayed. This is especially true in a monastic or intentional communal setting.

Even beyond that, sometimes I am just too tired to pray. At those times I have found that I can just lean on the structure of the Divine Office and Mass, and these will carry me. Sometimes praying the Divine Office or attending Mass can initially seem like a burden or an infringement on my private prayer inspiration or time. But I have found that while embracing this discipline might seem a bit limiting at times, it provides much welcome support when I am tired and weak. I have often not wanted to attend liturgy. But I have never left a liturgy without receiving a gift from God.

Then there is the hermit dimension. I have found that praying the Divine Office daily for thirty years has given me a discipline that also carries me now that I am in the hermitage more exclusively. In my religious reclusion I pray the Office with the community from the privacy of my hermit's cell. Through the years of praying the Office with community in choir and on the road the words have soaked deeply into my soul. They are almost second nature to me now. When I now pray them alone in solitude they take on an extraordinary dimension for me. I often find myself reduced to tears as I pray these most familiar words. Without the thirty years of training I am not so sure that they would touch me so deeply now. For this I am most grateful.

Do we take advantage of the gifts already given us in Christ and the church? Or do we sometimes try to reinvent the wheel? Not only is this unnecessary, it is very exhausting! Pick up the Liturgy of the Hours, learn how to pray it online or with a group of others in community, and sit back and soak in the riches of the ages. If you resist and complain, it will be a terrible burden. If you let go and let God, it will relax you and refresh you as a gift from God. If you set aside the place and time, it will take you beyond space and time with its ageless beauty in Christ.

Lay Prayers

The lay [brothers], however, shall pray twenty-four Our Fathers for Matins, five for Lauds, seven for each of the hours of Prime, Terce, Sext, and None, twelve for Vespers, and seven for Compline. And they shall pray for the dead.

It could be easy to skip over this little section of Francis's treatment of the Divine Office because our situation is so different today. But it still has significance regarding the different needs of the average laity and "professional" religious folks today.

In Francis's day most laypeople could not read or write. Only clerics and some of the nobility were educated enough to follow along with the prayers of the church in Latin. This meant that the lay brothers in the community needed a Divine Office that could be committed to memory. Francis used the common version of lay prayers consisting primarily of a repetition of the Our Father and some added popular prayers.

Though he called himself illiterate, Francis could read and write. He probably received an education from the cathedral school in Assisi, so he would have had the equivalent of today's eighth-grade education or so. Francis was ordained a deacon in order to preach to the people during liturgy, so he was considered part of the clergy, though he always identified most closely with the lay brothers. Though he could receive a larger clerical tonsure, he always preferred to receive a simple lay brother's tonsure.

In the desert most early monks were laymen and laywomen, not part of the clergy. Yet they prayed all 150 psalms every day. They committed them to memory, so they did not have to rely on books for common services. In order to learn them they presumably had to be able to either read or have someone teach them the psalms by rote. We know that St. Pachomius had all new members learn how to read as part of their novitiate. So lay monks in the desert were not entirely illiterate and prayed the entire Psalter in what we now call the Divine Office.

Today most everyone reads and writes and is fairly well educated. Most everyone can pray the Office once they learn how. Today the trick is learning how. The various page flipping required with the Roman Breviary is confusing to the average person trying to learn at home. Though there are internet programs that simplify this very well, the best way to learn is usually by participating with a community already praying the Office. It keeps the transmission of this knowledge human and alive. After a while it all becomes second nature.

But this can also be discouraging. Many Franciscan communities pray the Office by recitation rather than by singing, and often at breakneck speed. They have their reasons for this, but for a person trying to learn about the beauty of the Office this can be a real turnoff.

Ideally, I recommend finding a community that sings the Office. Benedictine monastic communities are great places to find this, but they use their own version of the Office, so it will not teach you to pray the Roman Breviary. I learned the structure of the Breviary from Franciscans and the beauty of the Office from Benedictine monks. We hope to combine the best of both here at Little Portion Hermitage.

For me this little addition to Francis's Rule regarding the Office also teaches another important lesson: not all people want, or need a complete experience of the Divine Office. Most folks are just trying to get through life as unscathed as possible. We love God, raise a family, and try to make a decent living. This takes up most of our time. Most people simply do not have the time to spend huge chunks of time and energy for religion. Some of us do. That is why we have monks, religious, and clergy. But the average Catholic Christian really only has time for brief daily prayers, and a Sunday or major feast day Mass at church. Only a few of the most "devout" make it to church more often.

So we need to find a way to pray that works best for us. It may be the full Divine Office, or it may be simple devotions. It may be meditating on the Scriptures of the day from Mass. What is important is that we pray every day. Usually twenty to thirty minutes in the morning and evening will do for most of us. If both cannot be done, I recommend the morning, for that sets the tone of the day. But if this cannot be done, pray in the evening or in bed before going to sleep. But do find time to pray every day.

I am reminded of a story about a great Catholic theologian. He has written many great works about highly intellectual approaches to God and the church. One day he was lecturing about the high mysteries of prayer and the like. But when one of his students asked how he himself prayed, he responded that he used the simple prayers taught to him as a child. What a wonderful lesson in simplicity and humility!

The older I get the more I realize that for all my study of Jesus, the church, monastic and Franciscan things, and mysticism and contemplative prayer, it is the simple truths of the faith that really get me through. The more I go into contemplative prayer the more I get out of the simple prayers, liturgies, and devotions of the church. I rarely have to go searching here and there for the deeper truths of Christ. They have been right there all along!

Fasting

And [all the brothers] shall fast from the feast of All Saints until the Nativity of the Lord. May those who fast voluntarily for that holy Lent which begins at Epiphany and continues for forty days, which the Lord consecrated by His own fast (cf. Mt 4:2), be blessed by the Lord; and those who do not wish to keep it shall not be obliged. But they shall fast during that other Lent which lasts until the Resurrection. At other times, however, they are not bound to fast except on Fridays. But in times of manifest necessity the brothers are not obliged to corporal fasting.

We Americans love to eat. Fast food and fine restaurants are more available in the average city now than ever before in our history. Obesity is no longer an oddity. It is an epidemic.

Fasting is one way out of this epidemic. Jesus fasted, as did the first disciples after Jesus' passion. The early church fasted on Wednesdays and Fridays. Those who desired to do so could also fast on Mondays. The Bible speaks of a great forty-day fast. Most of us can only go three days without water and survive. Solid food is different. This cannot be done too regularly, but in the case of an occasional fast, you can go longer periods of time without solid food. After three or so days the body will complain that it needs food, but it is not really in need of solid food yet. You are only breaking the habit pattern of daily food. In the case of an annual or biannual fast, most folks can go three or four weeks without food, or even forty days, but after that you must eat, or you will starve to death.

Francis followed a program of fasting for a serious religious person of his time. Personally, he took fasting to an unhealthy extreme. When they recently exhumed his body, his bones revealed that one of the reasons for his death was probably malnutrition. Francis was an extremist and confessed that he had abused his body before he died. Yet, he was moderate and charitable when applying fasting to his brothers. He always wanted moderation and mercy to rule in ascetical disciplines so that love, not extremism, would be the motive and mode of fasting among the brothers.

Written records of monastic fasting in the West date back to John Cassian, who brought the monastic practices of the desert monks to the southern coast of France. He recommended moderation in fasting. He said that extreme fasting often has the opposite effect. In other words, you overeat at the end of the extreme fasting period and end up committing the sin of gluttony rather than overcoming it. Moderate fasting every day is healthier. It helps us to overcome the vice of gluttony.

Following in that tradition St. Benedict allowed at least one red-meatless and uncooked meal a day even during times of intense fasting. On ordinary days he allowed two meals a day, one cooked, and one uncooked. None but the sick and the weak were allowed to eat red meat.

Fasting seems an almost small and unnecessary thing. What is really wrong with eating and drinking when God gave us these means of overcoming starvation? It is small, but it is not insignificant.

John Cassian echoes the entire monastic tradition of the Middle Eastern deserts when he lists gluttony as the first of the eight major sins. He also includes it as one of the three out of the eight that lead to the others. Gluttony is a small sensual sin that, if left unchecked, leads to greater sensual sins such as sexual sins. The principle is that a small sin can lead to a big sin if left untreated. He says that you overcome gluttony by moderate fasting.

The meditation masters of the Far East say that if one can learn to control one's breath then one can learn to control the other less basic sensual urges. The same is true of fasting. Eating and drinking is one of our most basic instincts. If we can learn to moderate our excesses in that area, then we can better learn to control our excesses with other more harmful abuses and addictions of our senses. Saint Francis's teaching on fasting carries this same message to anyone seriously willing to give it a try.

Are we addicted to food and drink? It is relatively easy to denounce the drunkard or drug addict. It is much tougher to denounce the glutton. The monastic definition of gluttony is eating or drinking when not truly hungry or thirsty. That's a pretty tough definition!

Are we quick to denounce the big sins, yet not willing to give up the small ones as well? It is easy to decry abortion or euthanasia or war in the name of being pro-life. It is quite another to give up the unequal distribution of the world's wealth that causes sickness, war, and death.

Are we willing to embrace a moderate consumption of food, drink, and all material things that is daily and steady, or do we engage in a futile series of stops and starts that eventually get us nowhere? Steady and even progress is better than grandiose measures that rarely accomplish much of anything in the long run. It is hard to "broad jump" into the kingdom of God. But if we take a small step day after day, after the course of a lifetime we will have traveled a long distance. The same is true of eating and drinking. Moderate, but serious fasting accomplishes greater goals in overcoming gluttony. Overcoming the little things leads us to the great. Slow but steady work in overcoming vice and living in virtue is the road traveled by most all the great saints.

Itinerancy

I counsel, admonish and exhort my brothers in the Lord Jesus Christ, that, when they go about the world, they do not quarrel or fight with words (cf. 2 Tim 2:14), or judge others; rather, let them be meek, peaceful and unassuming, gentle and humble, speaking courteously to everyone, as is becoming. And they should not ride horseback unless they are forced by manifest necessity or infirmity. *In whatever house* they enter, let them say: *Peace to this house* (cf. Lk 10:5). And, according to the holy Gospel, they are free to eat of whatever food is set before them (cf. Lk 10:8).

Francis simply assumed that the brothers would travel. Because they imitated the life of Christ and the first disciples as literally as they could, they had "nowhere to lay their heads" and spent their lives wandering from town to town administering the love of God. Jesus stood squarely in the tradition of homelessness that was common among the monastic movements of the religions of the East.

Hindus had four stages of life: the first was one of religious training under a master; the second was marrying, raising a family, and contributing to the economic good of society as a householder; the third was when a husband and wife had raised their children and felt called to greater religious observance by living in a hermitage as "forest dwellers"; and the fourth, and highest, was that of the sannyasi, or the renouncer, who wandered on foot in poverty in silence, begging his meals from day to day, and sometimes engaging in spiritual teaching. Sannyasi stayed in deserted caves, cemetery grounds, or forests, avoiding all signs of wealth or pride. After centuries many people wanted to go right to the fourth stage after the first. The Buddha was one of the most well-known of many such examples.

Jesus and his disciples fit pretty squarely into this itinerant tradition, though adapted to their culture and religion. But the church soon settled into fixed geographic communities of common life, such as in Acts 2 and 4, and finally into a more normal life of private property and such as described in 2 Corinthians 8. Monasticism of any religion began much that way, but also settled down into fixed hermitages and monasteries for large numbers of monks and nuns. This is a common pattern.

Francis and the first few friars attempted to return to the earlier model. In the beginning this worked well, but Francis also needed places to pray in seclusion and silence. These were the first hermitages, and Francis founded many of them. As more and more people joined the movement the friars also began to settle in larger convents in cities and towns. This gave rise to debates about poverty and prayer among the friars and led to reforms that attempted to return to the beginning charism of itinerancy and hermitages once more. This pattern has repeated many times in one form or another throughout Franciscan history. It is still going on today. But regardless of these reforms, all Franciscans have maintained an itinerant minister's life and can be sent from one friary to another in order to bring the gospel of Jesus to all people.

The main quality of this way of life is one of humility and poverty of spirit fostered by radical external poverty. They are to be instruments of peace. The friars are not to engage in needless debates and arguments or look down on either the rich or the poor. They are to remain lesser brothers and sisters, little brothers and sisters at the service of all. They can, however, defend the rights of the poor when necessary, as did St. Anthony of Padua. But all too easily this way of life can degenerate into religious pride that looks down on those who do not share it, live up to it, or agree with it. This is not the way of St. Francis. The divestiture of possessions in strict itinerant life is an aid and symbol of the divestiture of self that releases us from the need to judge others in order to justify ourselves. Otherwise our exterior poverty is just an egocentric sham. Then itinerancy becomes a source of shame.

We live in a highly transient world today. The average American only stays in one place for little more than four years. This can be highly destabilizing to families, workplaces, and communities. God knows that we need to learn the faith, hope, and charity that build greater stability in our families and communities that bring greater stability to the human psyche as well. This will bring spiritual, emotional, and mental healing to countless lives.

But it can also be an opportunity to learn the imperma-
nent nature of this passing world. The only thing that really
lasts and is eternal is God and the eternal things that flow
from him. The human spirit and the gifts of love will remain
forever. As it is commonly said, "Here we have no lasting
home." Nations will pass away. Even human marriages and
families will be absorbed into a greater spiritual family and
more intimate relationship with all that exists in heaven.
These things are eternal. Itinerancy and even the current
transience in Western society can remind us of these things.

But there is another lesson here as well. Can we see the
itinerant Christ and all his saints in the transient poor in our
midst? Today there are countless street people and immigrants in our midst. For many of us they remain nameless
and faceless "things" that populate our city streets, work
our agricultural fields, and do menial labor in factories. Yet
we cannot exist without them. Plus, if the Scripture teaches
us to be hospitable to strangers because in so doing many
have "entertained angels unawares," how much more is
this true of Jesus who was a homeless itinerant minister?
In some mystical way it may well be Jesus, and the many
saints of old that we encounter in the transient poor of our
culture.

How do we look upon our own impermanence? Do we see
it as a curse or a blessing to help us see our true and eternal
home? How do we look upon the transient poor among us?
Do we see them as valuable human souls or as necessary
but faceless "workers" in the fields of the modern manual
labor force? We must be a bit careful. Sometimes it is the
itinerant Christ and his saints who walk among us there.

Poverty

Chapter IV
The Brothers are never to receive money

I firmly command all the brothers that they in no way receive coins or money, either personally or through an intermediary. Nonetheless let the ministers and custodians alone take special care to provide for the needs of the sick and the clothing of the other brothers through spiritual friends according to [diversity of] places and seasons and cold climates, as they may judge the demands of necessity; excepting always, as stated above, they do not receive coins or money.

Francis is known for his extreme and rigorous poverty. It was so rigorous that his own brothers often found it difficult to embrace. It has continued as a source of debate and reform in the Franciscan family throughout the eight centuries of its history. Yet without it St. Francis would never have been such a free saint. It remains one of his greatest gifts. Without his approach to gospel poverty there is simply no St. Francis. And without him, there is no Franciscan family.

But Francis's approach to poverty was not born in a vacuum. It was born firmly from the religious and secular environment of his own time and makes perfect sense when seen in that context. This, in turn, helps us to apply it to our context in a credible way.

The religious environment of Francis's day was a time of intense reform. There were popular religious movements embracing radical poverty popping up everywhere. Some were wholesome. Some were not. All sought to observe the literal poverty of Jesus and the first disciples in a time where such radicalism had all but died out in established monastic communities. The penitential movement included itinerant preachers and hermits who lived in radical poverty. Communities like the Cathari or Waldenses were among those who were hostile to or splitting from the church in protest to her accumulated wealth. Other groups like some of the Poor Men of Lyons remained Catholic. The eleventh century had seen monastic reforms attempting to regain the early poverty and simplicity of the first monks of the desert. Francis stood squarely in this movement without breaking away from the church. What made him unique was his intense loyalty to the church born of radical humility, and a charismatic quality that made him most popular among those seeking similar reform.

The secular situation was also most interesting. It explains Francis's often misunderstood prohibition against even touching money. The secular world had moved from a system of bartering with the use of money as a way to augment and balance exchanges to one of an almost complete use of money. This newly emerging capitalism coupled with a new democratic government of local villages and cities was nothing short of revolutionary. It meant that those of the lower servant class, the minors, could potentially pass to the higher ruling class, the majors, through hard labor and becoming popular enough to be elected into local leadership. The old feudal system of hereditary lords and serfs with no possibility of really bettering oneself was passing away. It was so revolutionary that the pope formally endorsed this new democratic capitalism in communes like Assisi as a way to bring greater freedom and happiness to the average person.

Francis's father, Pietro Bernadone, was one such man who had made his way through the cloth business and married a higher-class woman from France, Lady Pica. But Francis saw that his father and many others were still enslaved to the fallen world through materialism even though they had made full use of this new economic and political system that was supposed to set them free. They were still essentially unhappy. So Francis gave it all up, intentionally embraced the life of the minor class, and lived a life of even greater freedom without ever even touching money. He showed everyone a greater way to freedom through a radical living of the gospel of Jesus.

Today this means that we would use serious discipline with something like a credit card to avoid the pitfalls of the delusional monetary freedom and terrible debt that the unwise use of credit cards has brought to so many. We might also unplug a bit from the addictive nature of the computer and the internet, which brings so much knowledge and communication but cannot offer real wisdom and face-to-face human relationships. On the religious level it means that we do well to stay on the cutting edge of the more radical spiritual movements of our day, but without falling into the religious pride that often accompanies them and causes their adherents to break away from the greater people of God of the church. Today, as then, Francis remains a radical but not fanatical example of how to live gospel poverty in a way that is relevant to our modern world. We need to conserve fundamentals without becoming fundamentalist in our approach to religion and life.

Daily Work

Chapter V
The Manner of working

Those brothers to whom the Lord has given the grace of
working should do their work faithfully and devotedly so
that, avoiding idleness, the enemy of the soul, they do not
extinguish the Spirit of holy prayer and devotion to which
all other things of our earthly existence must contribute.
As payment for their work they may receive whatever is
necessary for their own bodily needs and [those of] their
brothers, but not money in any form; and they should do
this humbly as is fitting for servants of God and followers
of most holy poverty.

Many people have a misconception about Francis. They
think that he only wanted the friars to beg. Not true. He
wanted the friars to work. If they could not find work, then
he wanted them to be humble enough to beg as all of the
poor of his day did. This would not be unlike being humble
enough to accept welfare or food stamps if one really could
not find a job today. I did this when I was young. I am sure
that some of you have as well. It takes swallowing your
pride, but it is what must be done in those circumstances.
But work is always the preferable option for the truly poor.

Saint Paul laid down the injunction that those who
would not work should not eat. Likewise, there is an old
teaching in the church from the *Didache*, or *The Teaching
of the Twelve Apostles*, that said if a prophet came to town
and did not minister his gift for three days, he should be

expelled as a false prophet. In other words, if he did not work for three days he should be expelled.

This became a universal rule in monastic history. The desert fathers taught that work was a major part of the monk's lives, and they spent much of each day doing manual labor such as making ropes. Some went so far as to unequivocally equate the life of the monk with work. Saint Benedict moderated but continued this teaching, and made daily work a valued part of monastic life. The work could vary according to each one's gifts, but work had to be done. Idleness was not an option.

Saint Francis continued this tradition as well. The first friars were sent to minister to the lepers as part of their novitiate training. Blessed Giles of Assisi was famous for his work ethic, and always found some humble manual labor to do even when being honored by staying in the houses of cardinals. Cardinal Jacques de Vitry even describes the early life of the friars as living in hermitages for contemplation, but close to towns and villages so that they could minister and work in them during part of the day.

At Little Portion Hermitage we always start new members in the farm with manual labor. It has a way of grounding a person in the simplest realities of life. Plus, quietly working with one's hands is some of the most contemplative work a person can do. It leaves the mind free to contemplate the things of God. After that, and after they grow in understanding our way of life, we begin to use their more specialized skills in other areas of our life and ministries. Only occasionally do we exempt someone from this rule of manual labor due to age or physical limitations. But most of us long for the days of quiet manual labor over life in a ministry office any day! If people are not humble enough to do this, then our way of life is not for them.

I am reminded of some of the candidates we received in our mission in Nicaragua for our monastic brotherhood.

Due to social classes and such those who are intellectually trained for church ministry are rarely from the poorer classes and consider such work beneath them. They simply refuse to do it. I was greatly disappointed when we encountered this.

I heard another statistic the other day. Fewer young people are working today than ever before in our nation's history. Nobody wants to do manual work anymore. Somehow young folks, and their parents, think that they are above such work. So they hold out for only the best paying jobs and will not work in the interim. We forget that Vatican II teaches the inherent dignity of all work, especially the hard manual labor. After all, this was the work of Jesus, the carpenter's son, before he began his ministry.

The other situation is with immigration, migrants, and undocumented workers. Since many young people will not do the menial tasks necessary for our society anymore, it falls to immigrants, migrants, and undocumented workers, along with the elderly, to fill the gap. I believe that such workers should be legally recognized, and should integrate into our society by learning the English language and such. But I also oppose those who protest their presence among us as "stealing American jobs." They are often doing the necessary work that those of us who live here are no longer willing to do.

Finally, there is the recent "recession," and the greatest financial crisis and loss of jobs since the Great Depression. Perhaps through this scourge on Western civilization we will be humble enough to be truly grateful for any work at all. The ability to work is a great gift, no matter how humble the task. We should not be humiliated by it. We should be honored by it, and be grateful to God for it.

Are we willing to work for a living? Or do we consider ourselves too good for it? Francis and the first friars considered work a special gift from God. They especially sought the most humble and menial tasks for themselves as a sign of the greatest service for others. Perhaps we, as followers of Jesus today, should learn something of their outlook and attitude.

Begging and Mendicancy

Chapter VI
The Brothers shall not acquire anything as their own; begging alms; the sick brothers

The brothers shall not acquire anything as their own, neither a house nor a place nor anything at all. Instead, as pilgrims and strangers (cf. 1 Pet 2:11) in this world who serve the Lord in poverty and humility, let them go begging for alms with full trust. Nor should they feel ashamed since the Lord made Himself poor for us in this world (cf. 2 Cor 8:9). This is that summit of highest poverty which has established you, my most beloved brothers, as heirs and kings of the kingdom of heaven; it has made you poor in the things [of this world] but exalted you in virtue (cf. Ja 2:5). Let this be your *portion*, which leads into *the land of the living* (cf. Ps. 141:6). Dedicating yourselves totally to this, my most beloved brothers, do not wish to have anything else forever under heaven for the sake of our Lord Jesus Christ.

To say that Francis wanted the brothers to work did not mean that he never wanted them to beg. Begging was the greatest act of communion with the poor. It was the greatest way to humility. He considered it God's special gift to the Friars Minor. Because they were God's beggars, they could not even consider the places where they lived as their own. Be they hermitages in the hills or friaries in the towns, they always belonged to someone else.

Religious begging is seen similarly in many cultures. In India the sannyasi are to beg as the highest expression of renunciation and union with God. Continuing that tradition the Buddha taught that the homeless monks were to beg every morning in a nearby town or village, return to their makeshift monastery or hermitage, and eat that same food before noon the day it was begged. Even after they had monasteries built for them by wealthy benefactors they continued this tradition.

Jesus was an itinerant minster who lived poorly off the alms of the faithful. He fits close to, but not exactly with, the religious mendicant tradition. The apostles pretty much did the same, but installed bishops in every local area. The early church also had itinerant ministers who lived off the alms of the faithful, as well as resident bishops and clergy who ministered to each local community. Monks tended to settle down in fixed places and do agricultural, intellectual, and spiritual work from these monastic religious centers.

Francis wanted to return to this itinerant gospel mode of life as literally as possible. So he wandered, worked, and begged. Even the first Franciscans eventually found that they needed some fixed places on earth in order to pray to heaven. But they tried to maintain this rule of never owning the places that they dwelled in. Though not always successful, it has remained an ideal, and a point of reform throughout the order's history.

Religious begging is not easy. Francis was ashamed to beg in Assisi at the beginning of his vocation, so he went to Rome and begged there. Once he got the hang of it he returned to his native city and engaged in begging. It is one thing to beg for stones to repair a church, but quite another to beg for one's own food and drink. Likewise, it is one thing to beg for the poor (I do this with Mercy Corps), but quite another to beg for one's own community. Often we have to go away to "get the hang" of our religious life before we bring it back home. Begging is symbolic of the more embarrassing things about one's own religious conversion and way of life. We have to be willing to give up the security of a respectable job and position to follow Christ. Only after we are ready to be a fool for Christ can we be ready for positions and ministries that bring some degree of worldly honor.

Probably the closest thing I have experienced to Franciscan door-to-door begging is modern door-to-door ministry. This means going out on foot from door to door in parishes that our ministry teams visit. At each door we simply identify ourselves as Brothers and Sisters of Charity who are ministering in the local parish and ask if they have any needs we can help them with or pray for. This ministry makes one very vulnerable because it sheds the safety net of a great plan or agenda. It is also not entirely flattering to one's spiritual pride to say that you engage in a ministry that will never get you famous or bring any notice to you whatsoever. Though I have sung before millions, door-to-door ministry is some of the most rewarding ministry I have ever done in my life. I almost never look forward to it. It is hard work. But I always return from it with one of the greatest rewards that earthly ministry can bring.

The Franciscans were part of a larger mendicant movement in the church at that time and were the main champions of it. Dominicans, Augustinians, and Carmelites were also mendicants. "Mendicant" means "openhanded." To be openhanded meant to ask for alms. It meant to beg.

But I like to think of another aspect of being mendicant, or openhanded. I ask people to sit in meditation and open their hands. In this action we release all that we are to God. We also open ourselves to others, especially those most in need. We give it all away. We let go of everything and all that we are. And in letting go of our very selves we discover who we really are. This is a profound way of opening our hands today that leads us to a great poverty. It leads us to poverty of spirit. This is the greatest poverty of all.

Are we openhanded or do we walk around with clinched fists? One way is relaxed and at peace. The other way is defensive and filled with self-preoccupation and fear. Open up not only your hands but also your entire life. Learn the gift of working for peace and realizing that any accomplishment is a gift from God. In this sense we are all "beggars." If you will do this then you will find the peace of Christ that surpasses all understanding. It is a peace that the world alone cannot bring by logic or politics or social action. But it is a peace that can heal the entire world on every level if we give it a try.

Family and Interdependence

And wherever the brothers may be together or meet [other] brothers, let them give witness that they are members of one family. And let each one confidently make known his need to the other, for, if a mother has such care and love for her son born according to the flesh (cf. 1 Thes 2:7), should not someone love and care for his brother according to the Spirit even more diligently? And if any of them becomes sick, the other brothers should serve him as they would wish to be served themselves (cf. Mt. 7:12).

This adds a beautiful perspective to the chapter on begging. We are to beg from one another with the confidence of asking one's mother for something we need. We are a spiritual family.

This builds not only on the language of the church who sees God as Father, Jesus as Brother, and church as Mother in the Spirit, but also on the entire monastic tradition. The early desert elders were called *abba* and *amma*, not because they were ordained priests in the modern sense, but because they were genuine spiritual fathers and mothers to their spiritual sons and daughters, or disciples. Saint Benedict calls the leader of his monastic community an abbot, or spiritual father. Saint Scholastica was an abbess, or spiritual mother, and the nuns (taken from the Latin word for grandmother) were sisters and daughters. Again, this was a spiritual designation independent of whether or not one might be an ordained cleric in the general structure of the church.

This means that all of us in the community are brothers and sisters in a very real sense. And no matter how upset we may sometimes get with our brothers and sisters, they remain our brothers and sisters for life and hold a very special place in our hearts. If this is true of blood family that is only for this brief life on earth, it should be all the more true of our spiritual family that is for all eternity. It cannot be undone.

It also brings out the interdependence of the community. We are dependent on God and interdependent with each other and all creation. None of us is independent. As

Scripture says, what happens to one happens to all. As St. Paul says, we weep with those who weep, and rejoice with those who rejoice. We are members of one another linked as a spiritual living organism through the indwelling of the Holy Spirit in us all. We are the Body of Christ.

The Scriptures also say that we are members of one another because we are members of the "body of Christ." The Holy Spirit dwells within us all, and unites us as one spiritual organism. We are literally part of one another on a spiritual level. Therefore if one hurts, we all hurt. If one succeeds, we all succeed. We cannot but affect one another. This is not some esoteric theory. It is spiritual fact. I am part of the person I dislike the most. I cannot just run away from them. They are part of me forever in Christ.

But the Spirit is everywhere because God is omnipresent, or present everywhere at once. Scripture even says that God is present in hell, as well as in heaven and earth. What makes his presence "saving" or not is whether one has a personal relationship of love with him. So we are interdependent with our immediate community, the entire church universal, all humanity and all creation. When rightly understood this is a revolutionary reality that cannot help but change the way we treat everyone and everything.

Do we treat others as part of our spiritual family? This is true of our specific community, our local church, the church universal, and of our earthly families as well. Do we try to ignore those we do not like? Do we try to pretend that they do not exist? But they do, and they will for all eternity. We will share that eternity with them in Christ. So we might as well get to know and love them now. Once we do, then we learn the secret of heaven, which is our ultimate eternal reality. We must learn it sooner or later, so we might as well get started now!

Penance and Forgiveness

Chapter VII
The Penance to be imposed on the brothers who sin

If any of the brothers, at the instigation of the enemy, sin mortally in regard to those sins about which it may have been decreed among the brothers to have recourse only to the ministers provincial, such brothers must have recourse to them as soon as possible, without delay. If these ministers are priests, they shall impose a penance upon them with mercy; but if they are not priests, they shall have it imposed by other priests of the Order as it seems best to them according to God. They must take care not to become angry or disturbed because of the sin of another, since anger and disturbance hinder charity in themselves and in others.

Francis called the Rule the "marrow of the gospel" and their way of life "the way of perfection." But the friars were far from perfect. Just like all other people, religious and nonreligious, they were sinners. As Scripture says, "All have sinned and fallen short of the glory of God." Sin is the great equalizer. So is forgiveness. None of us gets anywhere in the spiritual life without the forgiveness that jump-starts genuine conversion.

Though this is a special emphasis of Christianity, this can also be seen in other religions. Judaism speaks of the need for sacrifice, atonement, and forgiveness. Hindus and Buddhists say that one's sins are forgiven through a simple act of devotion that leads to real conversion from sin.

Though the monastic way in most religions offers a way of greater perfection, it also deals with sinful monks and nuns. Buddhist monasticism's legislation has page after page of how to deal with various major and minor sins. Only a few require the expulsion of an individual from the monastic community.

Benedictine monasticism is similar. Throughout the Rule of St. Benedict are references and some entire chapters dealing with sinful monks. This includes a wide variety of penances, ranging from eating separate from the rest of the community to corporeal punishment considered normative in society at the time. Though some of this may sound harsh to modern ears, at the time it was considered a most moderate and forgiving approach. It also brings out that every possible means was to be used to help reform a sinful monk. Only as a very last measure was one dismissed from the community.

Francis's Rule is similar. Mercy and forgiveness are to be shown. He spends one entire chapter addressing it. He also drops the reference of the earlier Rule of 1221 that automatically excluded a friar caught in fornication from the community (something the Buddhist monastic rule does). Apparently Francis had found that one could be brought back to righteousness and the authentic way of the Friars Minor even from grave sins.

But tangible penances are also given as aids in overcoming sin. It is usually not enough to simply say you forgive someone. Some guidelines must also be given to actually help the forgiven out of a sinful pattern of life. In modern times we sometimes call this tough love. But tough love can sometimes degenerate into hard-heartedness in the name of God. This is an ancient problem predating the title of tough love.

So Francis also warns that we are not to get angry over another's sin. Then we can be better equipped to really be merciful and forgiving with a sinner, no matter who they are or what they have done. We are to be merciful, and bring the forgiveness of God to the erring sinner. In another place Francis goes so far as to say that a sinful friar should be able to be called back to forgiveness only by looking into the eyes of the superior. This is quite remarkable.

I wonder if sinners are called to the love of God by looking into my eyes at such times? This is also pretty tough! The only way I know to do this is by first completely letting go of my egotistical need to be "right," even about religious things. Then I can bring God's love to an erring brother or sister.

Do we get angry when others "sin"? Often it is we who have sinned. If we seek God's will for others instead of our own will, then when others sin we only feel compassion and love. Yes, that love may have to be tough at times, but God help us if we are only tough without love. Often we only try to impose our own will in the name of God by quoting Scripture and church teachings. But despite its religious "clothing," such an approach is really only trying to impose our will onto the will of others. When we "let go, and let God," then his will is truly accomplished. Then love is free to flow to all of us everywhere. This is the most powerful in heaven and on earth.

Confession and Spiritual Direction

> If these ministers are priests, they shall impose a penance
> upon them with mercy; but if they are not priests, they
> shall have it imposed by other priests of the Order as it
> seems best to them according to God.

The Friars Minor lived in an interesting time when it
came to confession. It was a time when the current practice of frequent reception of the sacrament of penance was
just being accepted and implemented. So, the question of
whether to confess to a priest was still very relevant. It is
also relevant today, but from a different pastoral angle.

Originally the sacrament of penance was only allowed
once in a lifetime after baptism. This was considered generous. The rigorists of the early church argued that if one
were really serious about being a disciple of Jesus, he or she
would not intentionally commit major sin after baptism.
But experience taught otherwise. Christians were sinners
just like the rest of humanity. Penance to test the authenticity of one's repentance and forgiveness to let go of past
sins were needed even after baptism. Slowly the practice
became more frequent, but only included major public sins
such as theft, known sexual sins, murder, and so on. The
local bishop imposed public penances. This was the custom
for the first millennium of the history of the church.

There was also monastic confession. This was a nonsac-
ramental confession made to a spiritual father or mother.
These were usually laymen and laywomen. One confessed
not only sins but also all of one's thoughts, including

temptations to sin. Thus, spiritual directors were able to apply preventive remedies based on a full knowledge of the penitent's spiritual life and the wisdom learned from their own experience as elders. This confession was usually frequent, daily, or at least weekly.

As this monastic confession spread from the Middle Eastern deserts to Europe, the Celtic monks especially put it into practice. The nonmonastic laity saw that it was a most effective tool and wanted something similar. The church eventually responded by adapting the ancient practice of the sacrament of penance for more frequent reception. Thus, the modern practice of frequent reception of the sacrament of penance was born and remained the practice throughout the second millennium of Christian history.

Francis allowed for confession to a lay friar if a priest could not be found. But he preferred confession to a priest of the order when possible. When not possible, friars could go to secular, or diocesan, priests for confession.

Today we have a dual system of sacramental confession to a priest and spiritual direction from either qualified clergy or laity, male or female. You can use a priest for both, sometimes consolidating both with one priest. Confession is for sins. Spiritual direction is for the overall process of one's spiritual life. Both involve preventive and curative corporeal and spiritual practices to help go forward with one's spiritual life. In sacramental confession these are usually called "penances."

It is not always easy to find a good spiritual director, and with the priest shortage, confession is not as easy either. It is important to find someone truly qualified. This means someone who has lived what they teach before they teach it. Seminaries and spiritual direction schools are helpful in ensuring this, but they are not foolproof. For spiritual direction I usually refer folks to a good monk or nun. A brother or sister from a nonmonastic community like the Franciscans, Carmelites, or Jesuits can also be good. New communities also are a good resource for directors who are trying to really radically live what they are teaching.

Francis preferred that friars confess to friars when possible. That is because their new community demanded that the ones guiding its members understood the life. One from another state of life, or even from another religious community might not be able to do that even if they wanted. No doubt, like understands like. Celibates are good for celibates and families for families. Active community directors understand the active life better than a cloistered contemplative, and vice versa. Men are often better for men and women for women. But this rule is not absolute. Sometimes a hermit can counsel a family member of either sex better than anyone from his or her own state of life or sex. There is also the danger of a community turning in on itself. Francis was very open to guidance from qualified persons from outside his new community. I believe that this kind of humility was his saving grace.

So we need to be patient with one another and with ourselves when we find ourselves still falling into sin even after a serious commitment to Jesus and the church. We also need to make use of the means given us by God through the church and our respective community tradition for forgiving and overcoming those sins as we go forward together in Christ.

Do we make use of the sacrament of penance and the gift of spiritual direction, or do we try to go it alone? I usually try to get to confession about once or twice a month. I seek spiritual direction that often as well. This has literally saved my life on more than one occasion. If we humbly recognize that we are sinners and need spiritual direction and help, then we become more patient with others and can help lead them to such graces as well.

Centralization and Spiritual Parents

Chapter VIII
The Election of the Minister General of this Fraternity and the Chapter of Pentecost

All the brothers are bound always to have one of the brothers of this Order as the minister general and servant of the entire fraternity and they are bound strictly to obey him. Should he die, the election of a successor should be made by the ministers provincial and the custodians at the Chapter of Pentecost, for which the ministers provincial are always bound to convene in whatever place it has been decided by the minister general; and they shall do this once every three years or at a longer or shorter interval as decided by the aforesaid minister.

The community of Francis was different from those of traditional monks in the West. Monks promised stability to a particular monastery, and pretty much stayed in that one place their entire lives. The abbot was the spiritual father of the community and stayed with the monks of a particular monastery. Each monastery was autonomous, though they all shared the same Rule of St. Benedict. Originally there was not a central leader for all monastic houses.

Francis's friars moved around from place to place throughout the world. This meant they needed leaders who were over territories rather than monasteries. These territories were called provinces, and the leaders over them were called provincials. These provincials were much like local abbots, except they were over a region rather than one large monastery. Since the friars traveled throughout the entire known world, they needed a centralized leader who was over every provincial and province and over every friar and friary. This leader was called the general, or overall, minister. He was the minister "in general."

The world of Francis was changing from the feudal system to a new system of economics and government. Under the feudal system most people stayed in their own general vicinity for most of their lives. The average person rarely traveled more than a few miles from home during his or her lifetime. Trade was done through the local lord. The average person traded through simple bartering, perhaps augmented by the use of some money to even out the trade. Under the new system the use of money became the primary form of trade, and businesspeople traveled throughout Europe on business. Europe was now on the move.

The church was reflecting that change. Where local leadership was more primary in the old world system, centralized leadership became more important with the new. Though there had always been one leader in the bishop of Rome, the office of the pope was becoming more important, and the church was becoming more centralized in the way it actually functioned. Pope Innocent III represented the pinnacle of this shift in the way papal authority was lived out. He was the pope of St. Francis.

The office of minister general was originally for life. This was because the minister general was considered not only an elder brother among brothers but also the spiritual father of the entire community because he was the successor to St. Francis. Francis also used the language of "mother" for the leaders. Whether they are good or bad, our parents are our parents for life. We might have stepfathers and stepmothers, but we only have one father and mother. Franciscan scholars have noted that Francis did not really change the ancient desert tradition of the *abba* (father) and *amma* (mother), but changed the way they functioned geographically. Within a short while this life term proved impractical. Francis was the undisputed spiritual father of the movement. But despite his vision that the minister general is for a life term, he resigned before he died. Those who followed could not live up to the fatherhood of Francis. Within a few generations it became practical for the term of the general to be for around six years. They could be reelected.

Even the traditional monastic communities have made similar changes. Benedictines now have an abbot primate over a confederation of federations and congregations of monasteries. Cistercians actually predated the centralized leadership of the Franciscans and other mendicant communities with an abbot general. The huge monastic empire of Cluny in the ninth and tenth centuries predated them all. But the autonomy of each monastery is respected, and, for the most part, each monastery still has its own abbot or abbess. Likewise, many monasteries have a restricted term for their abbots and abbesses, though they can be reelected. Some have retained the original concept of a life term abbot or abbess.

For us this is relevant in several areas. We are an even more transient people than those of the time of Francis. For us, general and centralized authority is even more important in order for our world to simply function.

On a political level the role of federal government is now stronger in the United States than ever before. This can be seen especially after the Civil War and the presidency of Abraham Lincoln. The union of once-warring nations in Europe is slowly coming together in the modern European Union. The United Nations is a reasonably viable organization.

On the religious level the role of the pope and various Vatican congregations and pontifical councils have become more helpful and necessary than ever. The pope is certainly far more visible on the world stage today. Pope John Paul II made this an almost irreversible trend for modern popes of our era.

But we are also emphasizing the role of the local, regional, and national leadership again. Political international organizations value the appropriate autonomy of various nations and states in their unions. On the religious level the national and regional conferences of Catholic bishops have become great tools to helpfully lead the faithful in a given area. The laity have a stronger voice than ever in the church, and democracy is far more at work in the actual functioning of the Catholic Church. Women have a greater role in church government and function than ever before in history. Other churches have made similar adjustments and changes. We see the need for both, so the monks and the mendicants have much to teach us today.

We are also in a time when the need for a spiritual family is becoming all the more important for many of us. Natural families are breaking down. The language of a spiritual father or mother, as well as brother or sister, is challenging. On one hand, it is difficult to use such language when one's natural father, mother, brother, or sister have abused or deserted us and the family has ceased to function. On the other hand, it is precisely because of this breakdown that such language is important to reestablish the beauty and stability of these roles in a person's life. It can be a powerful source of healing. This is a great challenge for those in authority to use their authority for genuine service of the community and everyone in it, rather than for personal gain or power.

Do we stand with our family or do we abandon them? Do we place ourselves under the healing guidance of elders, spiritual fathers and mothers, or do we rebel against authority because of past failures and hurts? The family of faith can be a place of healing in Christ for those who are willing to humbly offer themselves to its healing hand and to remember that even leaders are human too! If we do this, then we can reach back out to the human family on all levels and bring the healing of Jesus to all others as well. Then both centralized and localized levels of political and religious organization will become channels of peace for the service of all humankind.

Democracy and the Chapter

Should he die, the election of a successor should be made by the ministers provincial and the custodians at the Chapter of Pentecost, for which the ministers provincial are always bound to convene in whatever place it has been decided by the minister general; and they shall do this once every three years or at a longer or shorter interval as decided by the aforesaid minister. And if at any time it should become evident to the body of the ministers provincial and the custodians that the aforesaid minister is not qualified for the service and general welfare of the brothers, then the same brothers, to whom the election is entrusted, are bound in the name of the Lord to elect another for themselves as custodian. After the Chapter of Pentecost each minister and custodian may call his brothers to a Chapter once in the same year in their territories—if they wish and if it seems expedient to them.

In most modern religious communities the supreme authority of that community rests with the general chapter. They can even remove a bad minister general in extremely serious cases, but not just because they may not like him.

Originally it was not that way. The history of most communities shows that they were usually founded by individuals that attracted groups, not by groups that raised up individuals. The Carmelites are an obvious exception to that rule; they were founded as a group of hermits on Mount Carmel and speak of several founders. Seven founders also founded the Servites. But normally this is not the case. A single person starts to live a radical gospel life and attracts followers. A community is formed, and governmental structures develop naturally under God's inspiration. Without these a community simply cannot function, even within the lifetime of the average founder.

The Rule of St. Benedict describes both an abbot and a chapter. Both are important. The "chapter" got its name from the fact that a chapter of the Rule of St. Benedict was normally read there. It is also where the normal business of the community was discussed and decided. The abbot does nothing of major importance without consulting the chapter. But the abbot has final authority. In the Rule of St. Benedict he was also to have a council of senior brothers to help in more mundane daily matters.

Today most communities have major superiors, like abbots, provincials, and general ministers, though the unique charism of each community colors the way that each is implemented. They also have chapters on the local, regional, and international levels. On the local level this usually involves the direct input of every member. Depending on the size, the regional chapters may be through delegates or directly with each member. On the general international level this is usually done through delegates. This is because direct participation by every member is impractical, so having elected representatives works out better, not unlike with a secular congress or parliament. They also have various councils at each level that work in union with the major superiors to help govern the community between chapters. The church is more monarchial than democratic, but even she is becoming more democratic in the way she functions. While supreme authority rests with the pope and the bishop of each diocese, ecumenical counsels, synods, and other gatherings are most important in discerning the "sensus fidei," or the sense of the faithful. Today this also includes gatherings and congresses of the laity as well as the clergy. But final authority still rests with the pope, bishops, and clergy. In the nineteenth century Cardinal John Henry Newman argued that even the infallibility of the church could not function unless the sense of the faithful of her members was not first discerned and seriously listened to. This was not always a popular position in Rome. But he has been proven correct.

So we need a balance between a primary leader or group of leaders, and the voice of the rank-and-file members of community. The members must seriously respect the spiritual father or mother and elder brothers and sisters, but these leaders must seriously listen to the voice of the people and serve them. Without this, leaders become dictators and democracies become mobs. These checks and balances bring about a community that is truly healthy.

How does this work out for most of us? We should first get involved in our local parish or religious community. This means being humble enough to follow appropriate leadership and to give our opinions humbly when asked for or appropriate. This kind of involvement is also possible on the regional, national, and international levels.

But to get involved we must also get informed. Many of us complain and voice our opinions about this, that, or the other in the church and the world before we have really taken the time to find out what is really going on, and what avenues for involvement are already open for us. Such investigation usually reveals that all kinds of opportunities exist for those willing to take the time to investigate and humbly serve.

This investigation also reveals that most of those involved are pretty dedicated folks. Maybe I am an oddity, but I have rarely met a major leader I did not like and could not respect. Most are far from perfect, but they are doing their jobs with the intention of real service of the people of God. They are usually far more saintly than I. I have also learned that they usually put me to shame in terms of service and experience. This makes me less apt to raise my voice in criticism or argument. It inclines me more toward listening, and loving and respectful dialogue.

So take the time. Find out about the issues and opportunities that exist for active participation in the church. It will lead you to a life of service and ministry that is most rewarding.

Preachers

Chapter IX
Preachers

The brothers shall not preach in the diocese of any bishop when he has opposed their doing so. And none of the brothers shall dare to preach to the people unless he has been examined and approved by the minister general of this fraternity and has received from him the office of preaching. I also admonish and exhort these brothers that, in their preaching, their words be *well chosen* and *chaste* (cf. Ps 11:7; 17:31), for the instruction and edification of the people, speaking to them of vices and virtues, punishment and glory in a discourse that is brief, because it was in few words that the Lord preached while on earth.

There is a popular quote going around today that is attributed to St. Francis, " Preach always, and if you must, use words." It is a beautiful quote. Unfortunately, Francis probably did not say it. It does, however, capture much of what Francis said about preaching.

There is such a story about Francis's approach to preaching from the early sources. In it he asks a young novice to accompany him into town to preach. The brother gets very excited. He gets to go preach with the famous Francis of Assisi! So off they go.

When they get into town Francis walks around and mingles with the shopkeepers and townsfolk. He greets people kindly and nicely asks how business is and so on. This goes on for some time. The young brother gets a little impatient waiting for the preaching to begin. Then Francis says, "Let's go home." The young brother cannot believe it. He asks, "But I thought that we were going to preach?" Francis responds that they had been preaching all day! Then the brother understood the deeper meaning of preaching.

This is not to say that Francis never wanted the brothers to preach. He just wanted them to be humble about it and to recognize that we preach all the time. Without the credibility of that witness all the great words in the world will fall on deaf ears. As Billy Graham says, unless the people of an area live credible Christian lives before he arrives, an evangelistic preaching crusade in a given area will always fail. Most of the early brothers were not preachers in the formal sense. They preached by their radical gospel lifestyle.

Those who did preach had to have permission to do so. They could not set out as self-appointed preachers. There were many such self-appointed preachers wandering around Italy in those days. Some were divisive and accusatory toward the church and those not leading the Christian life. Some were well-intentioned but unprepared for the ministry and ended up doing more harm than good.

Francis did not want to do even more harm, so he submitted himself to the guidance of the church, and asked his brothers to do the same. At first the friars were given permission to preach simple sermons about virtue and vice and a life of devotion and prayer. But they could not preach or teach theology. That required more study. Francis was not big on theological study because he had seen so many theologians and preachers lose their humility and faith in the simple gospel through worldly wisdom in God's name. But he was not totally opposed to good theology as long as it did not extinguish the humble spirit of devotion and a life of virtue.

Those who were presented to preach had to submit themselves to the discernment and guidance of the church and the order about these things before doing so. They had to be orthodox in doctrine and skillful in the art of preaching. Once a gift for this ministry is discerned, it can be honed and perfected by Spirit-led training and guidance. On the other hand, too much mere human training and guidance can also destroy it so that the original gift from God is lost. The balance has to be just right.

This training and guidance was a test not only of their orthodoxy and skill but also of their humility. Without humility a preacher is just a motivational speaker who happens to preach about Jesus. He is, as St. Paul says, "A clashing cymbal, and a noisy gong." Such preaching is often just enthusiastic entertainment in the name of Christ rather than preaching truly anointed by the Spirit of Christ. Sometimes we think that we are inspired, but we are just excited. Sometimes we think that we are called, but we are just driven. This can still involve a lot of ego.

I am reminded of the example of St. Anthony of Padua. He was the first friar Francis allowed to teach theology to the other brothers. He gave this permission because St. Anthony was humble, and he felt that a devoted prayer life and a life of virtue must precede the gift of preaching.

Saint Anthony was trained in theology and preaching as an Augustinian canon before he became a Friar Minor. One day he witnessed the first five Franciscan martyrs passing through town on the way to preach to the Muslims. Soon after he saw their dead bodies come back through. He joined the Friars Minor and first tried to be a martyr. When that did not happen, he settled into a humble life at a hermitage.

There he quietly went about the contemplative life, and served the other friars in ordinary domestic duties. They did not even know that he was a priest. When a bishop was passing through town it fell to the Franciscans to preach the homily at Mass. All excused themselves because they were afraid of making fools out of themselves. Finally it was decided that Anthony should do it because as the simplest one of all, he had nothing to lose. He preached the homily. Lo and behold, it was the best homily that anyone, including the bishop, had ever heard. They found out he was a priest, and his preaching ministry began. In many places he was more popular than St. Francis himself. So one of the greatest preaching ministries in church history began from real humility and a hidden contemplative life.

What about us? Are we willing to preach with our lives rather than with our words? Or do we feel the need to always voice our opinions and preach to others? Only when we are willing to be silent can we safely preach. Let's learn to listen before we speak and to quietly serve before we preach. Then we might be able to preach with the real anointing of the Spirit of God and really reach the people with God's word.

Missionaries among Muslims

Chapter XII
Those who go among the Saracens and other nonbelievers

Those brothers who, by divine inspiration, desire to go among the Saracens and other nonbelievers should ask permission from their ministers provincial. But the ministers should not grant permission except to those whom they consider fit to be sent.

Francis

Saint Francis wanted to reach out with the authentic good news of Jesus Christ to the Muslims of his day. This is most relevant for our situation with the rise of Islam today. His situation was very different, but there are still lessons to be learned that can help us as we face our challenges.

Francis had several reasons for going to the Holy Land to preach to Muslims. He did not believe that the sword could convert the people of Islam. He wanted to go armed only with the Spirit of God and with the Word of God. He even said that military strength against Islam would fail. This took great courage, and it took great faith. His prophecy was right. He eventually met the sultan of the armies of Islam. The sultan went so far as to say that if all Christians were like Francis he would convert and gave Francis safe passage anywhere in the Holy Land. Francis only returned home to deal with the troubles facing the community concerning the interpretation of the Rule.

Raymond Lull

The next figure of great relevance in Franciscan history is Raymond Lull, a lay member of the Brothers and Sisters of Penance, sometimes called the Third Order, and today called the Secular Franciscan Order. He also believed that only dialogue could win the hearts of the Muslims. He spent nine years in a hermitage on Mount Randa preparing for his ministry. He learned Arabic and studied the Koran. He went to the pope and religious orders such as the Franciscans and the Dominicans to establish a school to train missionaries to go to the Islamic world in a peaceful way. He eventually died a martyr in his ministry to the Muslims.

Fundamentalism

Today we cannot assume that all Muslims are moderate and peaceful people of faith. The modern problem is not with moderate Muslims, but with fanatical and fundamentalist Muslims. Fanatical Islam is a real threat to world peace today. The likes of Osama bin Laden and Al Qaeda do not represent the vast numbers of more moderate Muslims who want peace and justice throughout the world. But because the others are more violent and dangerous the moderates do not get the attention of the press. We sometimes forget that the moderates are there. But the numbers of the fanatical fundamentalists are growing. This is troubling.

And fundamentalism is a problem not only with Islam. You can find fundamentalists in every major religion. There are fundamentalist Christians and Jews. There are fundamentalist Hindus and Buddhists. And yes, there are even fundamentalist Catholics! Wherever it exists it tends to be triumphalist and exclusive. It is almost always the same internal creature, but it hides under different religious clothes!

But what is fundamentalism? I believe that it is taking a good fundamental of faith to an undue extreme without understanding its original intent or deeper meaning. It is often a reaction against a perception of a failed liberalism and is an attempt to "get back to basics." It can have religious, political, and cultural expressions. In religion this often leads to exclusivism and intolerance of anyone or anything that does not agree with one's take on the "true faith." In other words, it is "my way, or the highway." This can be a very scary thing.

Fanaticism

Related to this is religious fanaticism. An early church writing called the *Didache*, or *The Teaching of the Twelve Apostles*, actually calls fanaticism a "sin." "Sin" literally means to "miss the mark." God knows that there are plenty of religious fanatics on the loose nowadays. Those who use angry slogans or plant bombs on buses or blow up abortion clinics in the name of legitimate pro-life causes are fanatics. They have clearly missed the mark of God's will.

Missionaries Abroad and at Home

But this chapter of the Rule applies not only to missionaries among the Muslims but also to missionaries everywhere. We are to bring the gospel of Jesus Christ to the entire world. This is the clear teaching of Jesus at the end of his ministry on earth. It is the great commission.

But missionaries are not to go forth with a triumphalist attitude that disrespects the faith or culture of others. Far too often Christian missionaries have simply called all other faiths "satanic" and become cultural colonialists.

The Second Vatican Council teaches very clearly that missionaries should first learn the language, culture, and religion of the people they intend to minister to. They must have great love and respect for them. We should incorporate all that is good from them in bringing the gospel to them. And we can incorporate all that is good in them in the cultural manifestation of the Christian faith as it takes root in a particular land.

The Catholic tradition teaches and encourages appropriate ecumenical and interfaith activity. Ecumenical refers to all expressions of Christianity, and interfaith refers to all religions. We affirm that all truth comes from God, and that all religions contain various degrees of truth. All religions contain "seeds of the Word." We affirm that all share in varying expressions of the inspiration of the Spirit in their faith, morality, and mysticism as found in their scriptures, their meditation and worship, and in their way of life. This takes on a special significance with the formal revelation contained in the scriptures of the Jewish people, and with Jesus Christ, the Word Incarnate. So we proclaim the fullness of God's formal revelation in Jesus and the church. We are cautioned not to lose that which is unique to Catholic Christianity in our ecumenical and interfaith dialogue. If not fully grounded in our own faith we can easily lose it when dialoguing with those of other faiths. This is not the goal of such dialogue.

This is not as condescending as it might first sound. Catholic Christians may claim to have the fullness of God's gifts, but we do not always use the gifts we have very well. Often we can learn from other faith traditions how to better use the gifts that we hold in common with them. This takes us past proselytizing to real dialogue. Dialogue means that we must really listen to others and be willing to learn from them. It is based on humility rather than religious pride. This leads to real evangelization, or the sharing of "good news."

There are two models from the past that did not always work very well. They are the fulfillment model, and the universalist model. The fulfillment model basically says that now that Jesus has come, all that has come before can simply be discarded. If not, it can be regarded as a tool of the enemy, the devil. The universalist model says that Jesus is just one of many ways to God, so it does not really matter much whether one accepts Jesus. Since all good things come from God, the idea that one must receive Jesus to know the fullness of God is false, or at least optional. Both of these models are flawed.

I teach the model of complement and completion. Jesus complements all good cultures and faiths that have come before, and he completes them. All that is good from them can be used to present the gospel, and all that is good can be incorporated in the gospel. His completion is not religiously self-righteous. It is a result of simply being the Paradox of paradoxes, and the Mystery of mysteries. He is the way, the truth, and the life that complements and completes the way, the truth, and the life of all faiths. This seems to strike a better balance that is more loving and fair.

Today we need an approach to those of other faiths that is complementary to all without losing the unique gift of Jesus and the church. As the world grows smaller through travel and technology we need mutual respect, love, and understanding if we are going to build up a more just and peaceful world. The days of exclusivism and triumphalism are long gone. Return to them will only bring resentment, bloodshed, and war. This must be our approach with those of all faiths, but most especially with the growing threat of Islamic fundamentalism.

How do we approach those of other religions and cultures? Are we ready to see the good in them before we try to convert them to our way? Are we threatened by them, afraid of them, and resentful of them? All of these things must be healed and left behind in the love and reality of Jesus before any real evangelization or missionary activities can begin. Perhaps that is why St. Francis did not want just anyone sent out as a missionary. He wanted them to be spiritually, emotionally, and intellectually ready for the cultures and religions they would encounter as they brought the gospel of Jesus to the entire world.

The Testament

Introduction to
the Testament of St. Francis

The Testament of St. Francis is a last reminder, admonition, exhortation, and testament to the brothers of the community he founded. He wrote it when he was quite ill, probably in September of 1226, just before he died on October 3. Such words are to be taken very seriously, for they are the last things people formally say on this earth. For Francis it was the last communication he had with the entire community that he founded around the year 1209. His life had been relatively short. But he had come like a flash of lightning from God with enough power to light up the sky and to power a spiritual movement for centuries. He changed the course of the history of Western civilization for the better.

Some have said that the Testament was a correction and substitute for the final Rule of 1223. This is not true. He held the Rule as the "marrow of the gospel" and a covenant of salvation for the brothers and sisters of his community. The problem was not the Rule. It was the way the brothers interpreted the Rule that caused Francis such grief.

From the very beginning some of the friars resisted Francis about his strict adherence to poverty. They even tried to get him to write the Rule for himself, but not for them!

It was only a voice from heaven saying that the Rule was from God and was to be lived literally without gloss that kept them in line for the time being. But it was not long until the same old problems began again.

Some of the early sources indicate that the resistance of the friars to the authentic life that Francis had passed on to them caused Francis great pain. He resigned his office of leadership after he became ill. But some intimate that he also resigned because of his humility in the face of his inability to convince the friars to faithfully live the life as he had inspired. Some have even intimated that part of the stigmata was due to the pain he experienced at the infidelity of his friars to the Rule. The truth of these intimations is really only known to St. Francis and God. We can only speculate.

Regardless of these speculations, it can be said that the Testament is an attempt by Francis to remind the friars about the early days of the order and an admonition and exhortation to remain faithful to those ideals. In it he talks about the ideals that inspired him personally, as well as the first simple brothers. It is simple, beautiful, and clear. It is a most precious gift from a spiritual father to his spiritual sons before he died.

The Testament ends with the specific instructions about this, saying the following:

> And let the brothers not say: This is another Rule; because this is a remembrance, an admonition, an exhortation, and my testament, which I, little Brother Francis, prepare for all of you, my blessed brothers so that we may observe in a more Catholic manner the Rule which we have promised to the Lord.
>
> And the minister general and all other ministers and custodians are bound through obedience not to add to or subtract from these words. And let them always have

this writing with them along with the Rule. And in all the chapters which they hold, when they read the Rule, let them also read these words. And I through obedience strictly command all my brothers, cleric and lay, not to place glosses on the Rule or on these words, saying: They are to be understood in this way. But as the Lord has granted me to speak and to write the Rule and these words simply and purely, so shall you understand them simply and without gloss, and observe them with [their] holy manner of working until the end.

Despite the beauty and clarity of the Testament, the history of the Franciscan Order has reflected great tension about poverty and prayer as described by the Rule and Testament. In the early days there was a division between the so-called Spirituals and Conventuals. The Spirituals wanted to live more literally as Francis did. They lived in little hermitages, did simple work among the poor or begged as poor folk, and preached simply to the people. The Conventuals lived in cities and had libraries for study to prepare for preaching and teaching. For this they needed money and larger convents. The Spirituals often fell into heresy because of their simplicity, and the Conventuals often lost sight of the original vision of St. Francis.

Saint Bonaventure was able to bring unity to the troubled new community. He saw the value in the fidelity of the Spirituals and in the theological balance and orthodoxy of the Conventuals. By prayerful listening and balanced action he was able to bring some unity. He was a master of integration. But even his unification did not last long.

The history of the Franciscan family indicates a pattern of laxity and reform to return to the original vision of St. Francis. Ultimately the reforms slip into the laxity they were established to reform. This pattern seems to repeat about every 150 years or so. This pattern can also be seen in most all other communities in the church in a way that is unique to their charism.

Today the Testament stands as a reminder for us to be faithful to the original spirit of St. Francis of Assisi or to the communities and movements we are a part of. Most of us are not members of the Order of Friars Minor or even of a Franciscan reform. But we are inspired by St. Francis, and most assuredly by the gospel of Jesus Christ. The Testament contains the ideals of St. Francis that stand as inspirations for all of us.

Most of us have had a vision and call from God. After a while we often stray. Like the first friars we also need an encouragement to reform and return to the original calling. On a general level, the Testament of St. Francis is an inspiration to remain faithful to our calling from God. His simple and clear reminder of the original vision and his admonition and exhortation to remain faithful to that vision is a reminder, admonition, and exhortation for us all to do the same in our state of life in living the gospel of Jesus Christ as well.

God Inspired Me

[God inspired me], Brother Francis, to begin to do penance in this way: While I was in sin, it seemed very bitter to me to see lepers. And the Lord Himself led me among them and I had mercy upon them. And when I left them that

which seemed bitter to me was changed into sweetness
of soul and body; and afterward I lingered a little and left
the world.

"God inspired me"

This is how Francis begins the first paragraphs of his Testament. He does not say, "This is how I decided," or "This is
what I wanted." He clearly sees his life as something that
God initiated, rather than as something he himself did.
Furthermore, he does not even say, "God called me," or
"God commissioned me." He does not dare to place himself
on the same level as the prophets or apostles. He settles for
a simple, "God inspired me."

To be inspired means to be filled with the spirit of another. "Spirit" means the "breath," or wind. The spirit is the
intimate breath of another. It is often experienced between
two lovers who talk quietly to one another face to face. Or
it is best experienced when simply gazing at one another
without saying a word. Yet in that gaze all is known that
needs to be known. It is face to face and eye to eye. It is soul
to soul, for the eyes are the windows to the soul.

This is what Francis experienced from God. He was inspired. He was "in" the "spirit." He was filled with God's
Spirit. He was in love. His lover was Jesus. He was beloved
by God.

Personal Penance

Francis was called by God to help rebuild the entire
church. But he does not dare to see it that way. He began
by rebuilding the church immediately around him. He rebuilt San Damiano stone by stone. He used the little things
that were close at hand, and he built one thing at a time.
Eventually the entire church was rebuilt.

He began with personal penance. He did not look to change others before he had gone through a rather complete change himself. It is only in later paragraphs of the Testament that he starts to talk about brothers, and then without claiming any importance or glory for himself.

Lepers

It is interesting that out of all the events and symbols associated with Francis's initial conversion, he chooses to mention his encounter with lepers in his last Testament. He saw this encounter with what most repelled him as that which most changed him and set him free.

The service of lepers was also an important part of the early Franciscan life and was part of their training. They were to spend part of their novitiate serving the lepers, the most unclean of all in his society. This principle has stayed with most Franciscan formation programs to this day.

But even with this mention of lepers Francis does not mention the legendary story of his encounter with the leper on the road outside Assisi. That might possibly exalt him too much. He simply says "to see lepers." He leaves it to others to tell the more famous tale. This is typical of the way of St. Francis.

Bitter to Sweet

The most important thing in this experience is that what had previously nauseated him became a source of sweetness. He begins the journey into the paradox of the cross. Here the bitter becomes sweet. Later he will find that poverty becomes his wealth, and the death of Jesus becomes his resurrection into a whole new way of living. This way of paradox takes an apparent contradiction and communicates a deeper self-evident truth. It is the way of mystery. It is the way of the mystics of any faith. Jesus is the ultimate mystery, for he not only teaches and practices this way, he *is* this way. He is the way, the truth, and the life. It is this mystery that we encounter in the Eucharist.

One of the primary definitions for the word "sacrament" means "mystery." In the Eucharist we move through and beyond the senses, the emotions, and the intellect into pure Mystery. As Francis encountered the lepers he began this journey into the Mystery. He found the real presence of Jesus in them as an extension of the real presence of Jesus in the Blessed Sacrament.

Leaving the World

As he begins this journey he is also led to "leave the world." Once the dominos of the logic of this world begin to fall it is only a matter of time before they all have fallen. As the paradox of the cross of Jesus becomes more apparent he finds that he can only be saved in the world by leaving the world. As Evagrius says, "Renounce all to gain everything." He also said that once we leave the world we are "separated from all, and united to all." Francis was discovering this for himself. We can too.

Jesus says that we are not taken *out* of the world, but we are not *of* the world. Saint John says that the negative things of the world are sensual lust, enticement of the eyes, and pretentious life. Saint Paul would call this "carnality," or the "natural person." The world is good because God creates it. What makes it good or bad is how we use it.

How do we "renounce the world"? If we are detached from everything, then we can use everything in a godly way. We are no longer enslaved by the world, but are free even while in the world. This is a positive renunciation. It is the renunciation of Jesus and the saints.

Do we wait for God's inspiration or do we forge ahead with our own will. As religious people do we sometimes demand our own will even when saying that we are doing God's will? Some people are called by God. Some are just driven. One is humble. The other is still driven by ego.

Have we learned how to embrace the "bitter" things in our lives as well as the sweet? Scripture says that God makes all things work for good in those who love him. Even in the "bad" things of life, God has a lesson for us if we learn to approach all things with faith, hope, and charity. When we know this we can embrace all things, the bitter as well as the sweet, and all will be turned sweet. Then we can be at peace. This is a great mystery, and it is found in Jesus who is the Mystery of mysteries.

Faith in Churches and Prayer

And the Lord gave me such faith in churches that I would simply pray and speak in this way: "We adore You, Lord Jesus Christ, in all Your churches throughout the world, and we bless You, for through Your holy cross You have redeemed the world."

Sacred Spaces

Many folks think that St. Francis was opposed to institutional religion with church buildings and sacraments and such. This is not correct. Saint Francis believed that God was everywhere, and he had a special love for creation. But he also had a great love for sacred spaces and the church that builds and maintains them.

The Rule of St. Benedict speaks of this reality very well. It says that we believe the presence of God is everywhere, but is especially present during the Divine Office, or Work of God, and that the oratory should be a special place for prayer.

Francis started his religious life by rebuilding churches. God told him to rebuild the church. In his simple humility Francis thought that God meant the dilapidated church of San Damiano in which he received that message through the old Byzantine crucifix that still hung within it.

There are a few Franciscan sacred spaces that stand out to me here. Francis had a great love for San Damiano, which he prophesied would become the home of a community of contemplative sisters. Later St. Clare fulfilled that prophesy with the Poor Ladies of San Damiano, who would eventually be called the Poor Clares. He also loved the church of the Portiuncula, or "The Little Portion." It was the first home of the brothers. It was patterned after the classical hermitage and also became the place of the gathering of the brothers called "The Chapter of Mats." In this capacity it was the base from which the ministries of the community went forth. He loved this hermitage above all others. He also loved Alverna. This was the solitary mountain retreat that Count Orlando gave to Francis for a more complete contemplation. This was also the place where he received the stigmata, or the marks of the cross of Jesus in his hands, feet, and side. Saint Francis also established hermitages all across central and northern Italy. Sacred places of solitude and silence were loved and venerated by St. Francis.

Where are some important sacred spaces for us today? Of course our local worship space is a sacred space. It is the place where the people of God join together for the most sacred thing we can do together: worship God. This is a far cry from the social gathering space that many of our worship spaces have become. Don't get me wrong. It is very important for the community of the people of God to have real relationships with each other. Otherwise the worship of the community becomes an empty symbol of community. But reverent worship is the most important thing that we do in our sacred spaces. We are sometimes losing this in American churches of all denominations. Catholics are not exempt.

It is important for us to have a place of retreat that is sacred for us. I recommend that the average person have a monastery or retreat center where they go once a year or so. These places have what the local church does, a worship space, a place to eat and socialize, and such. But they also have an atmosphere of more intense sacred silence and solitude.

I also recommend a sacred space in our places of residence. A prayer room or prayer corner for prayer and meditation is very important for getting twenty to thirty minutes a day. Out of this twenty or thirty minutes a day we will probably get about two or three minutes of quality contemplation. This will be enough to get us through the normal ups and downs of an entire day.

Some people use nature as their sacred space. An isolated place in a woods or park can work for this. Some folks find great interior solitude and silence while walking or running. This is good for both body and soul. But this really cannot substitute for a more intentional stable place for meditation and prayer.

Simple Prayer

For all the greatness of St. Francis as an "alter Christus," or "another Christ," he never laid down a method or system for contemplative prayer. His prayer was very simple, but the biographers attest that Francis experienced the greatest contemplative heights possible. As with all the other aspects of his religious life, his humility led him to the greatest glories possible on this earth in Christ.

Even with the great teachers of contemplative prayer, the experience itself is beyond complex theories and methods. Contemplative prayer builds on sacred reading, vocal prayer, and meditation, but surpasses them all. These tools are good and even necessary, but they are just tools. They are not the actual experience of God. It builds on the asceticism of the senses, and the stilling and directing of thoughts and emotions. But contemplation is beyond all images, forms, or ideas. It can only be known through pure spiritual intuition. It is pure experience. It is pure union with God, spirit to Spirit, and essence to Essence. It is utter simplicity.

Yet there are some simple prayer tools out there. The first is the ancient practice of *lectio divina*, or sacred reading. The later monastic writers such as Guigo the Carthusian wrote of reading, vocal prayer, meditation, and contemplation. The first two have to do with our senses; the third includes thoughts and emotions; and the fourth uses pure spiritual intuition. *Lectio* amounts to a slow and prayerful reading of Scripture or sacred texts. Vocal prayer means to say the words out loud or to form them with the lips. This causes us to slow down our reading and allow them to sink more deeply into our consciousness. Meditation is the use of imagination to discipline our thoughts, and channel the emotions. After that we almost effortlessly pass over into contemplation beyond all senses, emotions, or thoughts.

The modern incorporation of seated meditation, where we slow our breathing to help us clear the clutter of unruly senses, emotions, and thoughts, is also helpful. Slowing the senses, emotions, and thoughts helps us to let go of the unruly patterns in these areas and allow new ones to emerge in Christ. This is especially relevant to the Christian's entrance into the cross of Jesus.

The Cross

This prayer of simplicity and contemplation is entered into through the paradox of the cross. The cross is the ultimate Paradox of paradoxes. In the cross we find life in death, wealth in poverty, communion in solitude, the word in silence, and the like. These paradoxes are an apparent contradiction that speaks a deeper truth. That truth is God.

Before the first brothers had money for prayer books, Francis taught them to pray this prayer: "We adore You, Lord Jesus Christ, in all Your churches throughout the world, and we bless You, for through Your holy cross You have redeemed the world." They were to pray it whenever they saw a church in the distance, a cross on a church, or even a cross in the branches of trees. They were also supposed to pray this prayer before the Blessed Sacrament.

In the simplicity of this prayer they could find some of the great mysteries of Jesus in the church. They were to enter into adoration. In adoration we allow the self to rise up outside of ourselves in order to lift up the One we love. Christ means the "anointed one" and calls us to be "Christian," or "like Christ," by also allowing the Spirit of God to anoint us. To "bless" means to extend all our best to another. When we bless God, we extend all that we are to God in Jesus. We empty ourselves of self in the self-emptying of Christ for the sake of Christ. The cross signifies that Jesus carries the sins of all the world in order to save the world. It also signifies that we realize our true God-given self by emptying ourselves in the self-emptying of Christ. It is by dying to the world that salvation is brought to the entire world.

Priests

Afterward the Lord gave me and still gives me such faith in priests who live according to the manner of the holy Roman Church because of their order, that if they were to persecute me, I would [still] have recourse to them. And if I possessed as much wisdom as Solomon had and I came upon pitiful priests of this world, I would not preach contrary to their will in the parishes in which they live. And I desire to fear, love, and honor them and all others as my masters. And I do not wish to consider sin in them because I discern the Son of God in them and they are my masters. And I act in this way since I see nothing corporally of the Most High Son of God in this world except His Most holy Body and Blood which they receive and which they alone administer to others.

Priests

Many people do not realize how much Francis loved priests. They see him as an anti-authority/institutional re-former as a precursor to the more anti-clerical expressions of the Protestant Reformation. But Francis had a deep love for both the church and her ministers.

Along with St. Benedict, Francis saw the divine in the human leader before him. Saint Benedict said that we must see Christ in the abbot. Francis saw this same thing in the leaders of the church. He submitted to popes, bishops, priests, and deacons, even when they were far less than perfect.

The early church had a leadership that included what today we call priests. In the Bible they are called "presbyters." Saint Paul instructed that bishops and presbyters be installed in every church they had established. Bishops were successors to the apostles and carried their full authority regarding the ministry of Word and sacrament. Presbyters carried certain aspects of the bishop's authority in what are called faculties. There were also deacons who preached the Word of God, and ministered charity to the local community. Ignatius of Antioch (the city where we were first called "Christians" and "Catholics") described the now normative threefold hierarchy of bishop, presbyter, and deacon for each authentic local Christian community.

Live According to the Laws of the Church

But Francis did not support priests indiscriminately. He says, "who live according to the manner of the holy Roman Church."

Francis lived in a time of great abuse by the clergy. It was not uncommon for the priests to engage in questionable financial dealings, as well as sexual immorality, usually keeping a concubine in absence of a wife. Then, of course, there was a general lack of spirituality and abuse of correct reverence in worship.

Many of the movements of Francis's day were trying to correct these abuses by a return to a radical and simple living of the gospel of Jesus Christ. They rejected the abusive lifestyle and practices of a corrupt clergy. The problem was that they often threw out the proverbial baby with the bathwater.

Francis differed from this approach. He believed in reforming the clergy, but not in throwing out the clergy altogether. In this sense he was more of a renewer than a reformer. He did not question the office of the priesthood. But he did question the abuses committed by the priests.

The way this lived itself out in practice was a public support of the clergy and a private ministry to the clergy to correct the abuses by them. Francis publically spoke of the great dignity of their office and ministry, but privately he would minister to them and even correct them. Most of the time this was done with great humility and discretion. Sometimes it meant a strong warning and rebuke. On some occasions this resulted in the priests losing their lives, and presumably their salvation. Such stories are seen in the lives and stories of the saints called "hagiography."

I think that this has special significance for us after the sexual scandals of our time. We now live in a society where sexual abuse of all kinds is alarmingly high. Pedophilia is proportionately even more evident in the general population than what we see in the church. Especially in the church, turning a blind eye to the sexual abuse of minors by clergy and laity is simply not acceptable. Along with millions of other good Catholics I am glad that the church has put proper checks into place to at least help prevent this crime in the future. But these are not perfect, and some priests have been irreparably damaged by false accusations, while others have still slipped through the cracks.

Church Persecution

In his day Francis took this support of the clergy to what many today would consider an extreme. He believed that you could best minister to the clergy by submitting to them. You could best lead them to humility by modeling humility.

Francis wanted the friars to obtain very clear permission from the local bishop before they tried to establish a hermitage or friary in any diocese. This is very different from some other saints like St. Teresa of Avila who often snuck into town in the middle of the night and set up a house and a chapel in order for their chaplain to offer Mass, thus making dismissal by the bishop impossible by the laws and customs of the day in Spain. This was a gutsy move to be sure and was even saintly. But it was not the practice of St. Francis. Francis's humility and obedience was a special gift that brought extraordinary results.

To use an Asian model, this is very Confucian. Confucius said that the best way to convert those over you to humility and service was by humbly serving them. The individual could convert the leader, who could convert the entire civilization. The younger could convert the elder, the children the parents, the wife the husband, the member the leader of the state, and the individual the state. For the Confucian the conversions rarely happened from the top down, but rather from the bottom up. This maintained the proper humility of the ideal person. The conversion may take longer, but it takes root much more deeply this way. Francis would have agreed.

Preaching

This obedience to bishops affected Francis's approach to preaching. He always wanted the friars to gain the permission of the local bishop and priest before any ministry was undertaken in a local area. This had special significance in the light of the fact that they had obtained papal permission to preach penance anywhere in the church. After his death the Franciscans actually were granted a papal brief to go into any parish church and preside at the Masses in order to preach and to minister to the people. They could do this whether the pastor wanted them to or not! Yet before he died Francis forbade the friars to use such papal briefs. They could only preach in a church if the local pastor had given his permission.

The Eucharist

Francis mainly honored the priests because he loved the presence of Jesus in the Eucharist. The presence of Jesus under the appearance of bread and wine in the Eucharist is "confected" by the Word of God spoken through the priest as God's established minister. The priest also touched the Eucharist with his own hands in order to bring it to the people. This made the priest holy, no matter how unholy he may have been personally before God. Again, Francis might have corrected that unholiness privately, but publically he always revered Jesus in the Eucharist, and in the priest rather than just revering a mere man or created elements. He was able to see God there because of his faith and the anointing of the Holy Spirit.

Today I often say that the music may be awful, the preaching terrible, and the people unfriendly. But if Jesus shows up at Mass, I guess I can too! Jesus always shows up through those very same people. Now, I really pray that music, preaching, and the Christian friendliness of the people gets better, but I am glad that this fundamental fact of our faith keeps the Catholic worship experience from becoming a personality cult where a motivational speaker substitutes real preaching and teaching, and a musical show substitutes for real sacred music. This also keeps the local parish from fragmenting into splinter groups every time the parishioners encounter a priest or lay ministers they do not like. It is an essential key to the phenomenon of unity that has persevered in the Catholic faith for over two thousand years. Francis understood this very clearly.

The Sacrament

And these most holy mysteries I wish to have honored above all things and to be reverenced and to have them reserved in precious places.

Francis lived in a time of renewal and reform. Liturgical abuses were rampant. Churches were often dirty, and the Sacred Scriptures and the sacrament were often kept in unsuitable places. The church had established reforms that instituted that the Scriptures and the sacrament be reserved in holy places set aside for holy things.

Interestingly, Francis began his vocation by rebuilding churches and cleaning existing ones. He was often found with a broom to sweep the dirt from the floors of churches. As Francis slowly began to realize, these things were all symbols of the inner rebuilding and cleaning needed in every human soul. Even less known to him was the rebuilding and cleansing of the church that God had in mind for Francis. This was all part of Francis's great humility.

The Blessed Sacrament

Some non-Catholics are a bit put off when they find out about Francis's great love and respect for the Eucharist. But there are some good reasons for it that are surprisingly closer to the hearts of other Christians than they may realize.

The first reason is simply environmental. The church of St. Francis simply took the reality of the Eucharist for granted. It was just accepted as a basic article of the orthodox Christian's faith. The only ones questioning that belief were those who were outside the accepted norm.

The second reason is more profound. The early church adhered to a belief in the Eucharist because of its more essential belief in the goodness of creation and the incarnation of God in Jesus. One of the movements challenging the authority of the church in the thirteenth century was Catharism. The Cathari were a thirteenth-century version of the Manicheans and some Gnostics of the early church. They believed that spirit was good and matter was evil. While the church believed that sin had compromised the original purity of the material world, she never believed that matter had become totally evil. The ramifications of such a belief eventually have dire effects on our stewardship of the created world. This ranges all the way from personal morality to ecology.

The church believes in the goodness of creation and in the divinity and humanity of Jesus. As the liturgy so eloquently states, Jesus took on our humanity so that we might share in his divinity. It also says that God created the world. Though it has been tainted by sin, it was redeemed in Christ and is in the process of experiencing that redemption through the actions of the redeemed.

The Eucharist is a powerful way to affirm these essential beliefs of the orthodox Christian faith. After the reforms of the church were instituted, St. Francis took up this banner as one of the main points of his popular preaching.

The Blessed Sacrament also takes us into Mystery. The heart of the gospel is not just a new set of religious ideas, good as those ideas may be. It is an actual experience of Jesus. It is a personal love relationship. This experience can be defined in part, but not completely. This complete definition remains beyond human ideas and words. It is a mystery, the mystery of love.

I have a dear non-Catholic friend who often says that at his church he experiences incredible music, worship, teaching, and preaching. The community prays fervently for those in need through petitions and intercessions. After this he feels really prepared to enter into the Mystery. He is ready! But just about then the pastor prays the closing prayer and everyone goes home. He complains that it is like being prepared for the mystery of spousal love and not being able to kiss the bride!

The Eucharist is the way for us to make the journey as a united people through senses, emotions, and intellect to the ultimate Mystery of God. We move from the knowable things of God to the Mystery that can only be known through unknowing. We make the journey from talking to God to being embraced by God. Both are necessary. In fact we need to communicate with words before we can communicate beyond words. The words help us define the definable so that we can establish and trust the authentic identity of each other. Only with this trust can we move beyond words into the mystery of love that defies all words. One is called orthodox doctrine, theology, and study and the like. The other is called pure contemplation.

Francis wanted the Eucharist suitably venerated and reserved in the churches of the friars. This helped firmly establish our modern practice of reserving the sacrament in suitable places in our churches as well.

Some question the more modern practice of exposition and adoration of the Blessed Sacrament. It is doubtful that this is what Francis is referring to. This practice developed later. There are reasons for this. First, exposition and adoration were established in a time when few people actually received Communion more than once or so a year. Exposition and adoration were ways to bring the faithful closer to the real presence of Jesus in the Eucharist.

Some would say that since we are now encouraged to receive Communion frequently, exposition and adoration are no longer needed. As they say, the Eucharist was established by Jesus to be consumed, not adored. True. But we are to consume the Eucharist with reverence. Plus, if we look down on past practices of infrequent Communion and exposition and adoration of the Blessed Sacrament, then we run the risk of the sin of pride. Nowadays there is probably room for both practices.

At Little Portion Hermitage we have found that there is truth in both. We receive Communion frequently and do not feel the need for exposition and adoration in order to be close to the Eucharist. But we have also found that exposition and adoration have helped us to focus our prayer in a very intentional way. We started the practice at the beginning of the first war in Iraq and have continued it for years.

The danger of exposition and adoration is that it can overly externalize our interior relationship with Jesus. Some folks spend hours before the sacrament, and receive Communion daily. Yet, they do not really have much of an interior life with Christ, and they fail to live like Christ when confronted with conflicts and challenges in daily life. Sometimes it seems that the more "religious" persons become, the more obsessive and judgmental they become, and the less like Christ they are in daily life. This is a tragedy that defeats the purpose of the Eucharist.

Church Decorations

Some folks mistakenly believe that Francis was opposed to nicely decorated churches. The opposite is actually true. He began his career sweeping out churches and making sure that Scriptures and the Blessed Sacrament were properly reserved and venerated. He also liked appropriate decorations that set aside special spaces as sacred.

Before Francis, St. Bernard, a leader of the Cistercian reform of the Benedictine tradition, had insisted on stark simplicity in Cistercian churches. All he allowed was a cross without a corpus. The walls were whitewashed and bare. This stark simplicity is quite beautiful and most conducive to quiet meditation.

Francis did not demand the same simplicity that Bernard did; therefore, Franciscan churches tend to be quite different. While retaining blessed simplicity, they celebrate the things of creation with wonderful splashes of color, sacred art, and symbols. Banners and stained glass will often tell the stories of Jesus, Scripture, and the saints for those not engaged in reading or in quiet meditation. Beautiful music lifts the spirit in the Spirit of God. Franciscans love contemplation beyond all images and forms. But they love the use of the images and forms of creation to rise above and enliven all creation in the love of God the Creator.

Do we make use of the images and forms of creation in our worship as we pass over into contemplation beyond all image and form? Do we make use of the various eucharistic devotions in a healthy way? Francis did both, and it brought him closer to Jesus. If done with faith, hope, and charity, it will for us as well.

The Word

Wherever I come upon His most holy written words in unbecoming places, I desire to gather them up and I ask that they be collected and placed in a suitable place. And we should honor and respect all theologians and those who minister the most holy divine words as those who minister spirit and life to us (cf. John 6:64).

The Eucharist cannot be "confected" without the Word of God spoken through the duly established minister of the altar. The Eucharist only makes sense in light of our belief in Jesus Christ. Jesus is the Word Incarnate.

To say the least, Francis was enthusiastic about properly reserving the Scriptures. Some would say he was downright fanatical! The Rule of 1221 says that whenever he found the Word of God, the name of God, or even letters that could spell the Word of God, he reserved them reverently in suitable places in churches. This was part of his ministry. He loved Jesus, and we hear the story of Jesus in the gospels. This meant that Francis loved the Word of God as it came to us in Scripture.

The love for the Word begins with a love for Jesus. He is the Word Incarnate. Some confuse the Word for the Bible. They commit the sin of what I call "bibliolatry." The Bible is only the written version of the Incarnate Word. The Word Incarnate is "in flesh," in "meat," in "carne"! This is a living Word that is proclaimed in speech and in silence. It is an evangelism that is active even in sacred stillness. This living Word is passed on person to person through the power of the Holy Spirit. This happened in an authoritative manner from Jesus to the apostles, and from the apostles to their successors in the churches they established. This is what we call apostolic succession, and is preserved in the bishops of the church, and in a special way with the bishop of Rome who is a successor to St. Peter who was given a special role of leadership in the early church.

The Scriptures are the written version of that more primary living Word. They come forth from the apostolic tradition of the church and for the church. They also reach out from the church to the entire world. The Scriptures are canonical. "Canon" means "yardstick." So the Scriptures measure all that comes after them. This does not mean that everything we encounter in life is found in Scripture. Rather, it means that the basic universal truths of the faith are found in Scripture. It is from these that we measure the things we encounter in life. Likewise, Scripture is "inspired," or God "breathed." It is without error regarding spiritual things, but not regarding other things. It is a spiritual book that includes history and science. Scripture is not a science and history book, and its strict inerrancy does not cover these areas.

Before Jesus, the Word was only seen in the written Word of God. Traditionally this originally was written most directly by the "finger of God" in the Ten Commandments and was continued through the writing of the history of God's special people and through the Pentateuch, the Psalter, the Prophets, and the Wisdom books of Scripture. After the time of Jesus, the Scriptures developed out of the life of the church and were established by the church. To understand the Scriptures we must understand something of the church.

Saint Augustine said that the Scriptures must be interpreted. It cannot be avoided. As soon as we read them we interpret them through the matrix of our own culture, time, and personal experience. He said that Scripture could be interpreted literally, symbolically, and spiritually for each person. Vatican II said that we must understand the history and spirit of Scripture before we can apply it to our lives. This means understanding both Scripture and apostolic tradition and its interpretation through the teaching authority of the church from which it came. Saint Bonaventure also said that we couldn't understand Scripture unless the same Spirit who anointed the writers and compilers of Scripture anoints us. This means being anointed by the Holy Spirit. Saint Paul says that the Spirit can be "fanned into flame." This is stirred up through public and private prayer. The church today wholeheartedly agrees.

Today this has relevance for the recommended practice of reserving not only the Blessed Sacrament but also the Sacred Scriptures.

In our hermitage chapel we tend to use a monastic set up. We place the ambo for the Scriptures at the entrance of the choir, and the altar at the far end. This brings out the relationship between the Word and the sacrament. We enter through the Word, but are led to the sacrament, the Mystery. The Eucharist cannot be confected without the Word of God. Yet, if we only have the Word of God we do not go forward to the mystery of the sacrament. We need both in our public worship and in our private prayer.

Theology

Related to his love for Scripture St. Francis also loved theologians. He saw them as the ones who unlocked many of the mysteries of Scripture for us. Francis tended to humble himself before all others, beginning with bishops, priests, deacons, other consecrated sisters and brothers, and theologians.

But he was very cautious of theology when it came to his own friars. He saw theology as a possible point of ego and pride for the theologians themselves. This was a common hindrance to the more primary call to prayer and devotion. For this reason he only allowed St. Anthony of Padua to teach theology to the first friars. Later, other teachers like St. Anthony would also be allowed by the successors to St. Francis and other legitimate major superiors of the order, and the Franciscan school became great unto itself among the other great religious schools. He knew that with a humble saint as a teacher it would be taught correctly. Only after they received this devotional training did other friars become theologians.

Sometimes we confuse theological study for authentic sacred reading, or *lectio*. We think that knowing about God is the same as knowing God. But it is not. We need some basic training in the context of Scripture in order to pray Scripture properly. But studying the Word of God is not the same as praying the Word of God. Study requires seemingly endless hours, days, and years of pouring over Scripture for its context and deeper meaning in a public setting. *Lectio* is a slow, prayerful reading of Scripture for a more private purpose.

And *lectio* is only the beginning of the process of prayer. After *lectio* comes vocal prayer, allowing the text to really soak into the consciousness. Then comes meditation using thoughts and emotions in a creative way. Only after this we pass over into contemplation that builds on but surpasses all words, images, and forms. This is the place of pure union with God that is spirit to Spirit, and essence to Essence. This is the final point and goal of all other forms of prayer.

Origen first used the term *lectio divina*. He did not use such strict definitions. For him it was just a prayerful reading of Scripture. It could include study as long as it was done prayerfully. It could also include the slower, prayerful reading of later centuries. I have drawn close to God through both. I am sure that Francis wouldn't mind. Do we have a balance between prayer and study in our life? Do we really love the Word of God? Do we spend time daily in prayerful *lectio* that leads into union with God? Do we do adequate study to at least understand the basics of theology so that we can enjoy the Scriptures without confusion? Francis was no Scripture scholar, but he understood the basics enough for him to have a lively prayer life that included a vast grasp of Scripture. Most important, all Scripture led St. Francis back to Jesus, who is the Word Incarnate, and the Holy Spirit, who writes the Word in our minds and hearts.

Community

And after the Lord gave me brothers, no one showed me what I should do, but the Most High Himself revealed to me that I should live according to the form of the Holy Gospel. And I had this written down simply and in a few words and the Lord Pope confirmed it for me. And those who came to receive life gave to the poor everything which they were capable of possessing and they were content with one tunic, patched inside and out, with a cord and short trousers. And we had no desire for anything more.

Francis never started out to found a community. He only wanted to have a relationship with Jesus. He began as an individual penitent. He became a hermit. He rebuilt San Damiano on his own. Then people came to join him. It was God who brought the brothers who formed the first community. Francis did not recruit them. Only after they came did he seek guidance about what to do with them.

In my own life as a founder I can relate to this. God gave me a vision of community. It was so beautiful that it seemed totally beyond my ability to found. I asked God what I was supposed to do. God said, "Stay in music, and I will open and shut the doors." I simply continued on my own life, and tried to grow closer to Jesus. Quite frankly, I made a mess of my life. Only after I ended up in a Franciscan retreat center, one or two people came to join me. I moved into a hermitage with the intention of staying there for a long, long time, perhaps even for life. Then God began to bring people who were somehow interested in what I was doing. Very slowly a community was formed. It was only after almost ten years that the community really began to take a form that was unique enough to call it a new form of community in the church. To try to get the cart before the horse would have been most presumptuous. It probably would have placed my soul in even more jeopardy than it would be as a founder. It also would have failed.

Toward the beginning of our life in community I wrote a simple rule. I suppose I have a need to organize things. As we progressed in the church it became apparent that something more specific would be necessary. I went to work with version after version of new "constitutions." (They say that all modern founders and foundresses are hack canon lawyers!) At that time my wife Viola challenged me just to do what the gospels said. So I wrote down a brief "Scripture Rule." Anyway, as time went on I discovered that it was better just to let the community unfold the specifics and to write it down after the life had taken shape. Soon enough we had a constitution and statutes that the church could approve.

Francis did pretty much the same thing. In the beginning he simply wrote down some Scriptures that were their "rule of life." He also placed himself under the guidance of the church. This happened first in the priest at San Damiano, then Bishop Guido of Assisi, and finally Pope Innocent III in Rome. Even in this he did not go immediately to the pope. He started right where he was, and worked his way along as it became necessary.

Community exists for a couple of reasons. The first is that community is a simple fact of life. Creation is a communal experience. Jesus says that when it rains both the good and evil get wet! Vatican II calls this "interdependence." As the old saying goes, "No man is an island." The second reason is that we are the Body of Christ. One member of the body supports and empowers the other members. Without community it is very difficult to persevere in the spiritual life, not to mention the specific disciplines of a particular religion. This is especially true of Christianity.

At the conclusion of my concerts I have the audience hold hands. We visualize that we receive Jesus in each hand. This is true in those who we think act like Jesus and in those who we think do not. It is only when we can find Jesus in others that we can give Jesus to others without being religiously self-righteous. It also means that when we are weak and cannot stand and walk, others will support us so that we can. We are to do the same with others. But we are not to drag others along. We are to firmly but gently hold others' hands, and genuinely help them to stand and walk again. This is the ultimate reason for community.

Simplicity

> And those who came to receive life gave to the poor everything which they were capable of possessing and they were content with one tunic, patched inside and out, with a cord and short trousers. And we had no desire for anything more.

The life of the brothers was very simple. More than a legalistic list of what they could or could not have, the Testament is a description of the beautiful simplicity of the life of the first friars. This simplicity gave them physical and spiritual freedom. As Francis said, the more you have the more you have to defend. As St. Paul said, celibacy is for the sake of the interior freedom of the celibate, not to place restrictions on people unnecessarily.

I can relate to the need to tell stories of the early days of community. In the beginning of the Brothers and Sisters of Charity we slept on mats on the floor. We made our own habits and we patched them when they wore thin. Our cells (rooms) were very simple, with a mat on the floor or a simple bed and a chair, plus a few holy pictures and books. Our common buildings were handmade and roughly decorated. Furniture was donated by the faithful. Televisions and media were minimal and used for religious purposes. We also went out on itinerant ministries in which we walked from place to place with no money or agenda. We simply offered our services at the local parish we encountered in exchange for food and a place to sleep. As we would say, we don't need to read the Little Flowers of St. Francis; we are living our own Little Flowers! It was a divinely enchanted time. We are still in our first generation, so we have maintained much of our simplicity. But even now we must remind ourselves of our blessed early days.

We always do best when we remain rooted in the simple foundations of our spiritual lives. As Jesus says to one of the churches in Revelation, you have developed well, but you have strayed from your first love. If we have strayed we can always return. Jesus never turns away from those who come back to him with an honest and sincere heart.

Simplicity

We [who were] clerics used to say the Office as other clerics did; the lay brothers said the Our Father; and we quite willingly stayed in churches. And we were simple and subject to all.

And I used to work with my hands, and I [still] desire to work; and I firmly wish that all my brothers give themselves to honest work. Let those who do not know how [to work] learn, not from desire of receiving wages for their work but as an example and in order to avoid idleness. And when we are not paid for our work, let us have recourse to the table of the Lord, seeking alms from door to door. The Lord revealed to me a greeting, as we used to say: "May the Lord give you peace."

This paragraph of the Testament rambles across some of Francis's favorite themes: the Divine Office, poverty, work, and poverty of spirit, or what we could generally call simplicity.

The Office

Francis says over and over again that he wanted the friars to pray the Office. He seems particularly intent on demonstrating that he and his friars were fully Catholic. This was in distinction to the other heterodox movements of his day. The Fourth Lateran Council of AD 1215 had mandated that clerics and religious should pray the Office as part of its liturgical reform.

The Franciscans had a big part in the development of what we call the Divine Office today. The monastic Office was based on the practice of the desert monks. Benedict adapted and integrated the monastic and the Roman Office into a workable and creative whole. These monks pretty much lived in one monastery their entire lives. The mendicants, like the Franciscans, traveled around the world. This affected their Office. While the monastic Office was rather lengthy, the Franciscans put together a breviary, or a brief version of the Office. As they traveled throughout Christendom they spread this breviary, and the clergy adopted it. The later Roman Office used aspects of this breviary that the Franciscans spread throughout Christendom.

Today's Office was further affected by the practice of the ecumenical community of Taizé. The earliest monks of the desert prayed all 150 psalms every day. The Benedictines moderated that to all 150 every week. The monks at Taizé reduced it to all 150 every month. The point today is to pray more with quality rather than mere quantity.

No Claim to Learning

Francis respected theologians and the learned, but he was skeptical of them as friars. This wasn't because he thought that learning was evil. He simply believed that learning often made one unhealthily self-sufficient. It caused one to think that he or she was superior to the unlearned and to mistake knowing about God for really knowing God. Both St. Bonaventure and St. Thomas Aquinas emphasized that the unlearned and the simple often knew more about God than did the theologians.

Francis called himself illiterate, but he was not. He probably received a typical rich son's education at Assisi's cathedral. This means he had the equivalent to what today we would call an eighth-grade education. He could read and write Latin and the local dialects. This placed him above the poor who did not benefit from any of these things. But he was not a university-educated man. He was no theologian, though theologians said that his theology "soared unto the heavens" while theirs "crept along the ground."

Today this is not unlike the difference that is sometimes found between the university-educated religious and the simple brothers and sisters. Very often it is the simple ones who manifest the greatest sanctity. The same thing is true of the laity. It is often the oblates and seculars who are the greatest saints in our midst. Some people used to call the Secular Franciscan Order the "Happy Death Society." But I have found that it is often the most quiet and least noticeable ones who are the real prayer warriors behind the more public ministers and monks of the church.

Francis was known as a great preacher and evangelist. But Francis said that it is not the preacher who converts souls, but rather the prayers of the humble lay brothers who live in the secluded hermitages in the woods who God honors by converting souls to Christ. Billy Graham has said much the same thing. He says that it is not his preaching that brings people to Christ, but the prayer and lifestyle witness of the local Christians who bring authenticity to his words. Only then can others believe the words of the preacher.

Work and Begging

Francis makes very clear his teaching about work and begging. The friars were to work. If they could not work, they were not to be too proud to beg. They were not to beg unnecessarily. But Francis did say that begging brought humility to the soul that no other action could bring. He also said that there was a special "contract" between the world and the friars. If the friars departed from poverty they broke the contract, and the world had no obligation to donate when they begged.

This was reminiscent of the religious begging of Hindu sannyasi and Buddhist monks who begged exclusively as their means of livelihood. Jesus also did the same thing. In return they were expected to pray and minister. If they departed from that authentic way of life, the laity was not expected to take care of them.

Today religious begging has taken on an entirely different form. Today we tend to do "appeals." These come via the mail, websites, or e-newsletters and e-mail. People are usually quite generous. But we rarely see friars going door-to-door to beg. Indeed, it is illegal in many local communities of modern society.

There is another form of begging in today's environment. This involves collecting unemployment benefits or food stamps or receiving other help via religious and charitable organizations. It takes great humility to take advantage of these things.

This has special significance in light of the recent economic downturn. As more and more people lose their retirement, jobs, and homes, there will be new forms of begging and giving. If Francis were alive today he would be found right in the thick of it.

Homelessness is the most radical modern expression of begging in the developed world today. These folks are not just freeloaders. They are lawyers, doctors, and other professional people who have lost their jobs, then their homes, then their spouses and cars. They end up on the streets. They say that most Americans are around ninety days from the street. Once you lose your job you are dangerously close to being unable to meet mortgage payments. The rest soon follows. I believe that if Francis were around today we would find him living part of his life among the street people.

Houses and Churches

Let the brothers beware that they by no means receive churches or poor dwellings or anything which is built for them, unless it is in harmony with [that] holy poverty which we have promised in the Rule, [and] let them always be guests there as pilgrims and strangers (1 Pet 2:11).

The early Franciscans would not accept money. Nor would they accept ownership of any place in which they lived, worshiped, or ministered. This was part of the gospel poverty they professed.

Prior to Francis the monastic communities accepted property as donations of land and buildings. Indeed it was necessary. Unless monasteries had buildings suited for their contemplative lifestyle they could not function well. They needed solitude and silence. They also needed a church, dining hall, and dormitories large enough to house the monastic community. Plus, they needed kitchens, workshops, scriptoriums to copy sacred manuscripts, and a guesthouse to minister to the constant flow of pilgrims that passed through monasteries, not to mention a space large enough to house the royal benefactors and their entire court as they traveled with royalty to visit their lands. Unless they had lands with villages, churches, and farms they could not support themselves. The villages, churches, and farms, all tithed to the monks. When used conscientiously, this system worked out well for everyone, but it could easily be abused by worldly monks, and abused it was.

Francis was humbly protesting the abuses of this system and the system itself. Part of this was subconscious. The world in which Francis lived was simply moving away from the feudal system that had built the monasteries of Europe. Most of the religious reforms at the time of Francis rejected any system that tended toward the accumulation of wealth. They did this in imitation of Jesus. Francis was no different, except that he embraced poverty without condemning the wealth of others.

In the beginning the friars stayed in places that were not their own. The sources describe them as staying in derelict churches, empty sheds, or even in abandoned ovens! They were itinerant hermit/preachers. They often rebuilt churches in the ancient laura and skete pattern of the monks of the desert. This amounted to a scattering of individual cells around a church and common building for prayer, meetings, and work.

The big thing was that they did not actually own their own places. They paid a rent of a basket of fish to the

Benedictine monks who owned the first place of the brothers, the Portiuncula, or Little Portion. Count Orlando "gave" them Mount Alverna for the more intense silence and solitude needed for contemplation, the place where Francis received the stigmata. These hermitages increased throughout Italy, and became the bases from which the various ministries of the brothers developed. Francis held these places in such great reverence that he told the friars that if they were driven out of the Portiuncula by one door, they should immediately come back in by another. But he always considered the ownership as belonging to someone else.

This gave precedent to an entire Franciscan system where the small and the great houses of the order were actually owned by a wealthy patron. Some friar preachers tended to preach in other parish and cathedral churches as itinerant ministers, but others started to build big churches at the friaries so that the friars could preach to large numbers at home. Bonaventure describes this in great detail and retains the original spirit of St. Francis. But the order did not always do so. In fact, it became just as corrupt as the feudal system of the monasteries that came before Francis. And reforms rose up from the ranks of conscientious Franciscans to return to the real poverty and prayer of the first friars. This is a pattern that repeats time and again in Franciscan history.

What does this say to us today? We live in a time when middle-class Americans have often built mansions in the suburbs. Mansions are crammed in one next to the other. They come complete with master-bedroom suites, his and her sinks, exotic showers and baths, luxurious kitchens and media centers, and on and on it goes. I must admit that these things are very nice, and I often enjoy them when I visit folks on the road. But the middle class is now enjoying an opulence that only the richest of the rich enjoyed not too many years ago.

The problem is that the banks own most of these. And the banks have often granted loans for folks to build these "mansion-strocities" when they could not really afford them. This helped lead us to the current mortgage crisis. Now we have banks going belly-up because they applied this irresponsible lending practice in big ways to major businesses, as well as to the average home buyer. Plus, good folks are losing jobs they thought to be very secure. This leaves many people in serious trouble paying their home loans, and houses are being foreclosed right and left. It is one of the issues amid a real economic crisis that is far more widespread worldwide.

Francis stands as a prophetic reminder that we need not be so greedy when it comes to housing. Something far simpler can do. Even then, by nature of the fact that we actually have a good roof over our heads, we are still in the upper 10 percent of the world's population. Compared to the majority of the world's population who live in dirt floor sheds, we are very fortunate.

It is said of Francis and the first friars that since they had nothing, they were everywhere at home. Francis also says that we really own nothing but our own sins. Our life, any goodness, and most certainly our possessions are all gifts of God. We only own what we negatively do with those gifts. If we realize that we do not really own our own home anyway, then we are not to be upset when we lose it. This results in the peace that St. Francis calls "perfect joy."

How are we doing in the housing mortgage crises? Does the loss of our job or our house cause undue instability? Granted, we are all upset. But deep down inside there can be a peace that passes all understanding that will get us through any loss. This is a peace that only Jesus can give.

Use of Authority

And I firmly command all of the brothers through obedience that, wherever they are, they should not be so bold as to seek any letter from the Roman Curia either personally or through an intermediary, neither for a church or for some other place or under the guise of preaching or even for the persecution of their bodies; but wherever they have not been received, let them flee into another country to do penance with the blessing of God.

Saint Francis and the first friars were given permission by Pope Innocent III to "preach penance." This is a very specific term. They were not given authority to teach or preach theological sermons. At that point most friars were laymen, and could simply exhort and encourage folks to "do penance" or to "turn back" to God. Francis was phenomenally successful, and he quickly became famous. Soon he was ordained a deacon in order to preach during the Mass, although Francis always identified primarily with the lay brothers.

Other friars also became successful preachers. Some were ordained priests and some were eventually elevated to bishops, though Francis originally taught that friars should not accept this honor out of humble caution about becoming proud. Saint Anthony of Padua is probably the greatest example of a famous preacher of theology in the first generation of friars. Saint Bonaventure comes to mind as a great teacher and bishop from the second generation.

As the generations rolled on the Franciscans were given great power in their ministries. At their height they could actually show up in a parish church and simply take over the duties of presiding over local liturgies and preaching! They were given papal briefs that empowered them to do so at their discretion. Of course the local bishop was consulted and worked with, but he really had to comply, and the parish priests did not need to be consulted and sometimes they weren't.

Francis did not want the friars to use this power, even though the pope himself granted it. He believed in working with local clergy instead of against them. He went so far as to say that if the local clergy did not want them to preach, then they should do whatever lowly ministry might be welcome. If even that was not welcome, then they should simply leave and not force themselves on anyone. If the local clergy persecuted them, they should gladly bear it for the sake of Christ. This was the way that brought greater peace to the friars internally, and to the local community. Division and dissent rarely bring the love of God. He also believed that you had greater effect when working with the local clergy, instead of working against or in spite of them.

A similar pattern is seen when teaching about ministering to the Muslims. Francis said that they could use two ways. The first was very direct. It was to preach Jesus openly in the streets. This way was open and clear, but it usually led to martyrdom. Its effects were immediate, but the fruit did not always last long. The second way was to do humble service among the Muslim people, and to seldom mention Jesus unless asked. This way had less-immediate effects, but the fruit often lasted a long time. The words were proved by loving deeds, so the words were spoken less, but had more effect.

The monastic tradition says much the same thing regarding their leaders. They are spiritual fathers and mothers. They hold the position of Christ to the community. They are "vicars." But they are taught to use their authority in a very gentle way whenever possible. Only when really necessary are abbots and abbesses to sternly use their authority.

The word "authority" is similar to our word "author." As an author I am most aware that I cannot write with authority about things I do not really know. I can quote Scripture or the life of a saint, but if I do not really know something of this reality in my own life I cannot write about it in a convincing way. We cannot have authority until Jesus has written his life and word on our heart. This is essential to the new covenant.

How do we use authority? Sometimes we are granted authority, but we actually lose moral authority by exercising it against the will of another. The leader must first be a good follower. The preacher must first be a good listener. The one who ministers in public must first be content with solitude. These are the paradoxes of the gospel of Jesus that authenticate the order and the church's great ministers and preachers. This is the real "authority" of Jesus.

Obedience, the Divine Office, and Discipline

And I firmly wish to obey the minister general of this fraternity and another guardian whom it might please him to give me. And I wish to be so captive in his hands that I cannot go [anywhere] or do [anything] beyond obedience and his will, for he is my master.

And although I may be simple and infirm, I wish nonetheless always to have a cleric who will celebrate the Office
for me as it is contained in the Rule. And all the other
brothers are bound to obey their guardians and to celebrate the Office according to the Rule. And [if] any are
found who do not celebrate the Office according to the
Rule and [who] wish to alter it in any way or [who] are
not Catholics, let all the brothers be obliged through obedience that wherever they come upon [such a brother] they
must bring him to the custodian [who is] nearest to that
place where they have found him. And the custodian is
strictly bound through obedience to guard him strongly
as a prisoner day and night, so that he cannot be snatched
from his hands until he can personally deliver him into the
hands of his minister. And the minister is strictly bound
through obedience to send him with brothers who shall
guard him as a prisoner day and night until they deliver
him before the Lord of Ostia who is the master, protector,
and corrector of the entire fraternity.

Obedience . . . Again

This is really just a recap of Francis's insistence that the
friars be humble religious brothers and obedient Catholics. Again, obedience is just learning to adopt a lifestyle of
listening. We start with religious superiors, and it spreads
out to all people and all creation. We learn to listen when
we silence the constant protestations and pontifications of
the inner ego and pride. When we do this we have peace.

Obedience is not only a fruit of this death to self and the
silencing of the ego. It is also a tool to help accomplish it.
Sometimes we have to bite our lip to keep from speaking
and putting in our two cents worth. It isn't easy. It even
feels unnatural at first. But if we will embrace a lifestyle
of silent listening we will soon be able to safely speak in a

way that is truly constructive and helpful. Obedience is a great tool to teach us this way.

The Divine Office

One of the ways to do this is to let go of our ego-driven need for novelty. The Divine Office is a discipline of the church that is ancient. It also helps us to embrace a way of prayer that is bigger than our own individual wants. It is also bigger than the wants of a particular group in only one place and point in time. It is the official prayer of the entire church universal, or Catholic. This prayer gives expression to the gathered people of the omnipresent God who spans space and time.

When we "get it," we begin to really enjoy the Divine Office in a whole new way. It ceases to be an obligation and becomes a privilege. It is not something we have to do, but becomes something we really want to do. It becomes a powerful experience that is much bigger than the normal ups and downs of any given day. It becomes a strength and anchor for every day. At least it has been that way for me. It seems that way to most who pray the Office in a meaningful way every day.

Punishment

Many of us today have real trouble with the more punitive language of monks and friars regarding obedience. Saint Benedict speaks of whipping disobedient brothers, and Francis talks about locking them up in a solitary cell. This seems most unchristian to modern ears. What is this all about?

Saint Benedict resorts to such measures only as a last resort before expelling the disobedient monk. Before that they are to use dialogue, encouragement, correction, and other lesser disciplinary measures. In a sense, Benedict says that we should use every available means to try to save the erring brother's vocation in Christ. After that, they can depart the monastery. Plus, they can ask to return after up to three expulsions.

In Benedict's day whipping was not considered extreme as long as it was done in a restrained and lawful manner. It was common in civil law and even in family disciplines. Today it would not be unlike using a psychologist as a last resort to try to help a monk with some kind of major problem. It seems rather "secular" to do so, but we should not be afraid to make use of this means if it might work. The aim is not so much the punishing of the monk, as it is the healing of a soul.

Francis's approach was not dissimilar. Locking a disobedient child in a cell in the basement of a house was perfectly acceptable discipline in the time of Francis. Francis was not afraid to use even this means if it might bring healing of soul to a disobedient friar. To understand this we must be willing to get beyond our twenty-first-century perspective, and see things more like Francis or Benedict saw things. This isn't easy, but it helps us to find the deeper lessons in even the more extreme things they seem to say.

Scripture says that God only disciplines the child he loves. If he didn't care, he would not go to the trouble or take the time to do it. But he does! Discipline teaches us that when we stray from the right spiritual path there is real danger and pain at stake. Like with our children, such discipline is a kind of practice for the real thing. A person who loves us administers discipline. It is for our own spiritual and temporal good. It is not meant to harm us. It is meant to help us grow spiritually in the way of Jesus Christ. Though for a different place and time, Francis's approach to religious discipline like this is administered for the same reason.

Are we willing to be corrected by God, the church, or spiritual leaders? If not, then we might want to do an ego check. We will not be whipped or locked up in today's churches or monasteries, but we will be corrected and disciplined from time to time. If we are never disciplined it is probably because the ones who lead us do not really care enough to take the time to do it. That is usually not the case.

Conclusion and Blessing

And let the brothers not say: This is another Rule; because this is a remembrance, an admonition, an exhortation, and my testament, which I, little Brother Francis, prepare for all of you, my blessed brothers so that we may observe in a more Catholic manner the Rule which we have promised to the Lord.

And the minister general and all other ministers and custodians are bound through obedience not to add to or subtract from these words. And let them always have this writing with them along with the Rule. And in all the chapters which they hold, when they read the Rule, let them also read these words. And I through obedience strictly command all my brothers, cleric and lay, not to place glosses on the Rule or on these words, saying: They are to be understood in this way. But as the Lord has granted me to speak and to write the Rule and these words simply and purely, so shall you understand them simply and without gloss, and observe them with [their] holy manner of working until the end.

And whoever shall have observed these [things], may he be filled in heaven with the blessing of the most high Father and on earth with the blessing of His beloved Son with the most Holy Spirit the Paraclete and with all the powers of heaven and all the saints. And I, little brother Francis, your servant, inasmuch as I can, confirm for you this most holy blessing both within and without.

We have already covered much of the first paragraph regarding the relationship between the Testament and the Rule of 1223 in the introduction to this section. What interests me here is the devotion the friars are encouraged to have toward the Rule and Testament. They are to hold them so special that that they are to be read in the meetings of the friars, called chapters. The chapter is a monastic term so called because at the chapter a chapter of the Rule of St. Benedict is read. Francis wants the Rule of the Order of Friars Minor read in a similar way. This places the Rule of 1223 on a most high level of respect. But not only the Rule, also the Testament. The Testament is an encouragement for the friars to stay true to the Rule in a Catholic way that does not rationalize away the meaning of the Rule. This means that Francis must have feared that the friars were already misinterpreting the Rule before his death. The early sources leave us no doubt but that they were.

A Franciscan Canon

Francis uses biblical language that emphasizes the importance of the Rule and Testament. He says not to add or subtract to the words of these documents. He says not to "add to or subtract from these words." This is the same language used by Scripture at the end of the Apocalypse, or book of Revelation. It is also used in the Old Testament at the end of the Pentateuch, or the first five books of the Bible.

This does not mean that the additional prophetic, poetic, and wisdom books of the Old Testament were offenses against that injunction. It only means that those first five books were to be held with special authority relative to all that would follow. The same is said of the New Testament concerning any noncanonical apostolic tradition that would follow.

For Christians the Bible is the canon by which any further apostolic development is measured. This does not mean that everything in the future must be explicitly contained there. That would be rather absurd. But it does provide a universal measuring stick with which to assess any further development. Francis indicates the same thing about the relationship of the Rule and Testament to any further development of the Franciscan tradition and lifestyle.

Blessing

Francis concludes with a blessing. A "blessing" means a prayer for "happiness." But it is not just any happiness. It is the happiness of what the Greeks called the "Blessed Isle." This island retains its happiness regardless of the peace or storminess of the sea around it. This is true happiness. It does not come or go based on mere external circumstances. It remains forever.

I am reminded of the story of the Perfect Joy of St. Francis. In the story Francis asks Br. Leo where perfect joy might be found? He asks if it is found in being so great an evangelist as to convert the multitudes, or in healing the people, or in being greatly learned and wise, and so forth. But Francis says that, good as those things might be, perfect joy is not found there.

He says that perfect joy is found in knocking on the door of the local friary after a long day's walk in the freezing rain only to be denied entrance. After knocking again and begging to be let in by your own brothers you are verbally abused. After knocking and begging once more, they come out and beat you bloody and throw you in the icy ditch. Francis says that perfect joy is found right there as long as one can keep one's inner peace even after the injustice.

This is quite a story, and quite a challenge. It means that when one really lets the old self of egocentrism die with Christ then we can rise up interiorly with Christ no matter what our outer circumstance might be. This is the central goal of the entire Franciscan way of life. It is the beginning, midpoint, and end of all things in the monastic way, the Franciscan way, and the entire Christian way. It is the paschal mystery, the dying and rising of Jesus Christ. It is this life that the Rule and Testament try to establish, maintain, and protect.

When we have this perfect joy of St. Francis then we are blessed indeed. We are the "Happy Isle," that is at peace no matter what storms may rise up in the waters of this world around us. The waters of our soul and spirit remain calm.

May we carry the Rule and Testament not only on our person and read it in chapter, but also in our hearts and minds at all times and read and meditate on its words and deeper meaning all the days of our lives. Then our entire lives will be blessed in Jesus and in the church.